Green Ivy Publishing

1 Lincoln Centre

18W140 Butterfield Road

Suite 1500

Oakbrook Terrace IL 60181-4843

ISBN: 978-1-942901-73-0

D1158578

CHAPTER 1

When Brenda and I first met and got married, producing a child with special needs was the last thing on our mind. After graduating high school, Brenda was very fortunate to land a job at the local medical clinic working as a receptionist for Doctor Russell. That is how we first met each other. I had sustained a very serious injury to my right knee playing baseball a few years earlier and occasionally needed to visit the doctor for problems I was still having with it. I was pleasantly surprised to meet Brenda when I showed up for my appointment. I really didn't know much about her except that she lived in town with her two-year-old daughter. I had known Brenda's parents for several years though and absolutely loved them.

Curiosity started to get to me after my appointment with Dr. Russell. It must of have been fate that Brenda and I eventually met on the parking lot of the local supermarket. I had seen Brenda driving towards me down the street in town and blinked my lights, signaling her to pull into the supermarket lot. How many relationships have ever started more romantically than ours? For us, it was a match made in heaven. We started dating in early February, got engaged in July, and married in mid-November. I remember my dad asking me if I knew what I was getting into. He told me that we were going to be an instant family. "Your first responsibility will be to the child, I hope you realize that. Gina will be number one in your new marriage, not you." My dad was right. We went through a big adjustment period as a new family. There was a big jealousy battle that started between Gina and me for Brenda's affection. Of course, my dad was right about this situation and I would be the loser. It was very sad competing against a two-year-old for the love of the same person. I needed to grow up.

When we found out Brenda was pregnant with Brett, things seemed to change. We all seemed to be on the same team. A new baby was going to change our whole situation, hopefully bringing us all together as one. Coming together as an everlasting team would be no joke. Brett's birth would change all our lives forever.

Brenda and I didn't realize anything was seriously wrong with our son Brett until he was around eight months old. Slowly, month after month passed with one problem turning into another. Brett was just over a year old when he was diagnosed with cerebral palsy. I remember the night Brenda told me the diagnosis. At first I was devastated. Then my reaction turned to denial. I had no idea what cerebral palsy actually was, but I knew my son didn't have that disability. How could such a cute baby have something wrong? He looked as normal as any other child his age. There is no way to describe the emotions I felt that night. I remember walking outside to get some fresh air. We had livestock that needed hay and water in our barn, along with a dog and several outside cats waiting for food. When I opened the door to the barn and turned on the light, all the animals were huddled together in a corner on the ground. It was a very cold evening, and this was their way of keeping warm. My emotions exploded as I climbed into the loft of the barn to retrieve some hay. I cried my eyes out for several minutes. On a scale of one to ten, this was the number one worst day of my life.

Brenda handled the situation very differently. She seemed to have that motherly instinct telling her something had been wrong with Brett for a long time. Her grandmother told her at lunch one day that Brett wasn't doing some things that normal babies should do at his age. Brenda felt responsible for his disability, and so did I. I remember so many late nights lying in bed next to Brenda, wondering why she was so restless. Some nights I could tell that she was crying, and when I would ask her if something was wrong, she would just tell me her allergies were acting up. I knew she was blaming herself, just like I had blamed myself for a long time after we learned Brett had a disability. We were both uncertain as to what was in the future regarding Brett's disability.

The burden of holding back these emotions started to show when Brett was around three years old. I could tell Brenda was upset about something one night as we were getting ready for bed. I could sense something was bothering her. I finally asked, "Did something happen today, what's wrong?"

She said, "It was just a bad day with Brett." She had taken Brett to several different medical appointments at the clinics that day. It was the typical trip endured several times a year, seeing doctors with different opinions on how to treat Brett. That day, for some reason, was very different. Something unusual happened and it was really bothering her.

Brenda asked, "Have you noticed when we take Brett to a new doctor, the first question they ask is what caused his disability? Why does your son have cerebral palsy? Why do they ask that question? Are we missing something? They think it's because of my blood pressure when I was pregnant. I just can't take it anymore! I'm the reason Brett has cerebral palsy!"

The same questions had been tormenting me since Brett was diagnosed with cerebral palsy. I said, "I've always blamed it on the decisions we made the night he was born, not on you, on us!"

"What are you talking about?" Brenda asked. "We had no choice. We did what we thought was right for our baby."

"Brenda, I've always blamed myself for being so stupid and not asking more questions about what was going on that night," I replied. "I had no idea you felt the same guilt all this time."

Brenda asked, "What are we going to do?"

I had always questioned the decisions made that night and the days after, but I kept it to myself. We made decisions with the information given to us at the time. We did what the doctor told us to do! I told Brenda, "I've always wanted to investigate what really happened to Brett but figured it would never change anything. Maybe we do need to investigate this to give us peace of mind."

"How are we going to pay for someone to investigate what happened?" Brenda asked. "We can't afford to pay for something like that. Are you crazy?"

"Let me make some calls at work tomorrow," I replied. "I think were entitled to some free legal consultation through the union."

When I called the union hall to inquire about legal consultation, they informed me we were allowed a thirty-minute free consultation and gave me the name and phone number of the attorney. When I called his office, the receptionist told me he was tied up in court for the rest of the day. She told me to leave a message on his voicemail, which took me by surprise. How do you place everything you need to say into such a short message? Here was my message:

> My name is Keith Meyer. I have a three-year-old son diagnosed with cerebral palsy. We believe mistakes were made in his care and would like advice as to what our options are. I would appreciate talking with you regarding this matter as soon as possible.

Driving home that night, I thought about everything I needed to gather up and organize before seeing the attorney. Most of the information was in my head, but I needed to find some pictures taken before and after Brett was born. I arrived home just before Brenda and the kids that evening. I noticed there was a message on our answering machine when I walked into the house.

> Mr. Meyer, thank you for calling my office today. I need to refer you to another attorney more specialized in medical malpractice cases. His name is James Stone. I talked to Jim about your situation, and he would like to speak to you at your earliest convenience regarding this matter. Good luck to you and your family.

It was only 5:15 p.m. I wondered if it was too late to call Stone's office. I went ahead and dialed the number.

"Stone, Charles, and Brooks," a voice said. I told the receptionist my name and explained that I had been referred to Mr. Stone regarding a legal matter concerning my son. The receptionist asked me to please wait one moment, and when Mr. Stone came onto the phone line he sounded very pleasant. We talked for several minutes about Brett and our situation. He asked if I could find time to come by his office, and I told him I was available any time after 3:30 p.m. most days.

"How does tomorrow at around 4 p.m. sound?" he asked. I said it sounded great and that I looked forward to meeting him.

When Brenda arrived home, I told her about my conversation with Mr. Stone. She was very surprised that I already had made an appointment to talk to an attorney. Brenda was starting to have second thoughts about the whole situation. "Are you sure about this?" she asked. "Maybe we should talk more before this goes any further."

"Brenda, we need to quit blaming each other about what happened to Brett," I replied. "We need to find out why Brett has cerebral palsy. This is not going to cost us a penny. Either way, by tomorrow night at this time maybe we will be able to start releasing some of the guilt we've put on ourselves for the last three years."

The next day I took a clean change of clothing for after work. I tried to clean up as good as I could after working all day in ninety degree heat. Driving towards Mr. Stone's office, I started to get nervous about what was about to happen. Brenda and I shared so much guilt for what happened to our son at birth. The only problem was that we didn't know what we did to cause Brett's cerebral palsy.

It only took me about twenty minutes to arrive at the address of the law firm, which was located on the ninth floor of a huge high rise building. As I walked from the parking garage into the building and towards the elevator, I could see myself in a huge mirror next to the elevator. Oh my god! I look like a Hoosier, I thought to myself. Oh well, too late to turn back now! Walking off the elevator and into Mr. Stone's office, I felt like I was walking into something you would see on TV. Everything was so shiny and fancy. I was really starting to feel uncomfortable about my appearance after working all day in the heat and humidity. I walked up to the receptionist and gave her my name. She said, "Mr. Stone is expecting you. I will let him know you're here."

As Mr. Stone approached to greet me, he looked professional, confident, and, unlike me, well dressed. He greeted me with a handshake. I followed him into a conference room where we began to talk. "How can I help you, Mr. Meyer?"

I started, "Our three-year-old son Brett was diagnosed with cerebral palsy just after he was a year old. We believe some wrong decisions were made leading up to and on the night he was born. We've been asked several times by different medical personnel what caused the CP. We placed the blame on ourselves for some of our decisions and for not asking more questions. Now I'm here talking to you, still trying to figure it all out."

Mr. Stone wanted some history about me and the rest of

the family. I told him that I had worked as a construction laborer for almost ten years and that Brenda was the receptionist at the medical clinic in a small town close to where we lived. Brenda and I had been married for over six years at that point. We lived out in the country on about four acres, which was a small part of several acres of farm ground owned by Brenda's parents. We purchased the house, barn, and machine shed from her parents just before Brett was born. It was a two story farmhouse that needed a lot of work, but we were so thankful to have a home of our own. We were the third generation of Brenda's family to live in the house. I had a seventy to eighty-mile commute each way to work every day. It was a lot of miles per week, but I loved living away from the hustle and bustle of the city.

"Is Brett your only child?" Mr. Stone asked.

"No," I replied. "We have an eight-year-old daughter. Her name is Gina."

"Are you her natural father?" Stone quickly asked.

"No, you're very observant with the dates," I responded. "Gina was two years old when I married Brenda. She was the flower girl on our wedding day. We were an instant family. I consider her my own daughter though, I love her very much. Gina is now in the third grade and doing very well. She and Brett are like two peas in a pod. Gina would do anything for her brother and treats him like he doesn't have a disability. That's a challenge for Brett, but it's good for him to be pushed."

"You mentioned Brenda works for a doctor," Mr. Stone said. "Did he treat her while she was pregnant?"

"No, he monitored her condition more than anything," I answered. "The OB doctor was really concerned about her blood pressure and wanted it monitored on a daily basis. She developed the problem just after giving birth to Gina."

Mr. Stone observed, "She seems very young to already have high blood pressure. Have they checked to see what is causing it?"

"Not really," I said. "I think it's hereditary. Her dad experienced the same problem at a very young age."

"Do you think the doctor Brenda works for would answer some questions regarding her pregnancy with Brett?"

"I…I don't know," I replied. I really didn't think Brenda would want him involved, especially when he didn't even know that we were investigating this. "Brenda is very concerned she could lose her job if word about this gets out."

Mr. Stone asked, "Did Brenda have any problems with Gina's pregnancy?"

"Everything went fine, to my knowledge," I responded. "I know Brenda went full term with Gina. She might have even gone past her due date a few days, I'm not sure. Gina was around seven pounds six ounces when she was born."

"OK, tell me about your son," Mr. Stone instructed. "How has the cerebral palsy affected his life?"

I leaned back in my chair and said, "Brett is three and a half years old. He is way behind other children his age, both physically and mentally. We are unsure about his vision. At first they told us he was blind, but we now know he can see certain things, we just don't know what. He has already had surgery on both eyes to correct some problems and tubes surgically installed in his ear for recurring infections. Brett still doesn't walk, but he crawls faster than some people can walk. We have been told that he will probably require surgery on his legs and ankles in the near future due to problems caused by the CP. Other than that, Brett is a very healthy and happy child."

"Have the doctors given you any idea about his life expectancy? Will his life be much shorter due to the cerebral palsy?" Mr. Stone asked.

"No, as far as I know he is as healthy as any other child his age," I said. "Whatever damage his brain sustained at birth will never get better or worse. I guess we really don't know. No one has ever told us what to expect when he gets older. At this point I honestly don't want to know. We have already endured a lifetime of problems it seems like, just in the first three and a half years. I'll stop right there, though. I've seen other people with more serious problems than ours."

"I imagine you have," Mr. Stone replied. "Do you have any thoughts as to what did damage Brett's brain at birth?"

"I think about it every day," I said. "Both Brenda and I have blamed ourselves for a long time over what happened when he was born. We think we should have asked more questions or made better... I don't know... It's a long story."

"Please tell me your story."

"Would you like the quick or long version?"

Mr. Stone smiled and said "I want everything."

"I can still remember the day Brenda surprised me with the news that she was pregnant," I began. "I remember it was a beautiful spring day. Brenda was so excited and looked so happy! Both of us were thrilled. She told me that the doctor projected her due date to be in the first week of February. I think February third was the exact day, I'm not sure. The doctor told Brenda he was going to retire soon and suggested she find a new doctor. I really don't remember much about him. The new obstetrician Brenda started seeing was Doctor Robert Hall. He must have just started his practice because all Brenda could talk about was how young and cute he was."

Mr. Stone cut in. "On what date did Brenda start going to Dr. Hall?   What was his projection as to a due date?"

"I think her first appointment with Dr. Hall was around the first of July," I replied. "He projected her due date to be the middle of January."

"So, between two doctors, we have two different projected due dates," Mr. Stone said. "How is it possible for two doctors to come up with such different due date projections? Please continue."

I continued. "I remember taking off work early one day to meet Brenda at Dr. Hall's office for an ultrasound. I'm pretty sure it was around the first of October because it was her second ultrasound as I remember. This was my first chance to meet Dr. Hall. He seemed like a great guy. Both Brenda and I were very comfortable around him. After his examination and the ultrasound, he asked to see both of us in his office. He told us everything looked great. He said the baby was at 24.5 weeks gestation and that we still had a long way to go.

"Brenda's blood pressure had been very borderline, and that concerned him. He was going to watch her very closely, and he wanted her vitals monitored on a daily basis at her office. If her condition changed, he wanted to be called immediately. In our case, he felt we had to make it to thirty-seven weeks. At thirty-seven weeks, the baby would be fully developed. If we didn't make it to thirty-seven weeks, he said our child would be premature and would probably need to be transferred to a facility better equipped to handle premature babies. If we did make it to thirty-seven weeks, which he was confident we would, he would make the determination on whether to continue or terminate the pregnancy at that point. In our case, he said he would probably induce Brenda or take the baby by C-section. The date we needed to shoot for was the week of December twenty-seventh, just after Christmas.

"Brenda and I left Dr. Hall's office thrilled with the possible chance of having a Christmas baby. I was excited thinking about getting that tax deduction if the baby was born before the end of the year."

Mr. Stone leaned forward and started writing on his legal pad on the conference table. "Let me think about this," he said. "The projected due date had gone from early February, to the middle of January, and then Dr. Hall said that he was not going to let the pregnancy go past the end of December, specifically the twenty-seventh. This is fascinating."

"I know, I was confused myself," I replied. "I do have pictures of the ultrasounds that were done. The first was done in September and shows the estimated gestational age at 20.5 weeks. The second was on the first of October and shows her at 24.5 weeks, and the third ultrasound was done on November twelfth and shows Brenda at thirty-one weeks." I leaned forward and handed him the pictures.

"Excellent. Can I hold on to these pictures?"

I said he could and then continued. "Everything went well for the next several weeks. Brenda used this time to finish up her Christ-

11

mas shopping as the Thanksgiving weekend approached. We had so many things to be thankful for. Thanksgiving was like the calm before the storm, though. Brenda seemed more stressed and irritable as each day passed. On November thirtieth, Brenda went to work not feeling well. She knew something was wrong. When Dr. Russell arrived at the office early that morning, she complained of experiencing a clear discharge the last few days with increased urinary frequency, and she hadn't felt fetal movement yet that day. Doc checked her blood pressure. It was elevated, and he immediately called Dr. Hall with her symptoms. After hearing what was going on with Brenda, Dr. Hall told Doc to send her to his office as soon as possible.

"Brenda called her mother to see if she would drive her because she didn't want me to miss any work time. Brenda and her mom, Vicky, both agreed I shouldn't be bothered at work until they knew something was actually wrong. When Dr. Hall first looked at Brenda at his office, he could tell something was wrong. After he examined Brenda, he seemed very concerned, and he wanted her to be admitted outpatient at the hospital for a non-stress test and other monitoring of the baby. He wasn't taking any chances. Brenda finally called my boss and told him she was in the hospital for tests and I should not leave work early but come to the hospital after I was off. When my boss gave me the message, I wasn't surprised. I had noticed Brenda seemed different the last few days.

"After work, I raced to the hospital. Since we had already been through maternity classes, I knew Brenda would be on the third floor of the hospital in labor and delivery. When I arrived at her room, I was surprised to see her in such good spirits after enduring such a stressful day. Vicky told me they were doing different tests to make sure Brenda and the baby were OK. She told me the doctor would be in later to talk to us. I thanked her for driving and staying with her all day, and Vicky left to pick up Gina at the babysitter and keep her until we knew something. Brenda was on her second non-stress test."

The fetal non-stress test is a simple non-invasive test performed in pregnancies over twenty-eight weeks in gestation. The test is named 'non-stress' because no stress is placed on the fetus during it. The test involves attaching one belt to the mother's abdomen to measure fetal heart rate and another belt to measure contractions.

Movement, heart rate, and reactivity of heart rate to movement are measured for twenty to thirty minutes. If the baby doesn't move, it does not necessarily indicate that there is a problem; the baby could just be asleep. The primary goal of the test is to measure the heart rate of the fetus in response to its own movements. Healthy babies will respond with an increased heart rate during times of movement, and the heart rate will decrease at rest.

The concept behind a non-stress test is that adequate oxygen is required for fetal activity and heart rate to be within normal ranges. When oxygen levels are low, the fetus may not respond normally. Low oxygen levels can be also caused by problems with the placenta or umbilical cord. A reactive non-stress result indicates that blood flow, and oxygen, to the fetus is adequate. A nonreactive non-stress result requires additional testing to determine whether the result is truly due to poor oxygenation, or whether there are other reasons for fetal non-reactivity.

"Both tests that were done on Brenda came back 'not reactive,' even after stimulation movement and eating and drinking cold fluids. I think we both started to stress at the same time that something was very wrong with the baby at this point. I'm sure my blood pressure was elevated enough to set off alarms—much less how Brenda was handling the situation.

"At that point, Brenda had endured blood tests, ultrasounds, and non-stress tests with no actual proof that the baby was okay or in distress. A nurse told us that Dr. Hall wanted to administer the oxytocin challenge test. It required admission to the hospital so they could induce Brenda to start having contractions to determine the baby's condition."

An intravenous solution of Pitocin is given very slowly until there are three contractions in a ten-minute period, and the fetal heartbeat is monitored electronically. A negative OCT is when there are three contractions in ten minutes without fetal heart decelerations. A positive OCT is defined as a test where more than fifty percent of contractions are associated with late decelerations.

"Brenda slowly started having contractions, and everything seemed to be going well. Dr. Hall entered the room just as Brenda was finishing some contractions. He watched the monitors for a minute, then studied her chart. He started to examine Brenda and asked her how she felt. She said she was tired. He smiled and said we were only at thirty-three weeks. He reminded us how crucial it was to make it to thirty-seven weeks. He said the baby was doing fine and Brenda's vital signs were looking a lot better than earlier that day, but we needed to treat her symptoms like warning signs. He said he had no choice but put her on strict bed rest for the remainder of the pregnancy. We had to do everything possible to make it another four weeks. If and when we made it to thirty-seven weeks, he would probably end the pregnancy by inducing her or taking the baby by C-section. Doctor Hall wanted her back at the hospital in a week for another non-stress test, and again every week after that. He also wanted her to call if she felt decreased movement or if her water broke. He said we both needed to take this very seriously. He expected me to help out around the house and make sure Brenda followed his instructions.

"As Dr. Hall left the room I could see Brenda's eyes begin to well up, and she began to cry. She sobbed that she couldn't take off work, that Doc wouldn't let her take off that long, that she was going to lose her job. I told her it was going to be fine. Doc would understand how serious this was. Brenda just shook her head as she wiped more tears from her eyes. After calling Dr. Russell, she felt much better. He told her not to worry about work and that she should take care of herself and the baby. He assured her everything would be alright.

"Everything went well for the next three weeks," I continued. "We were up to thirty-six weeks and still hanging in there. I did what I could around the house in the evenings after work and on weekends to keep things caught up. Brenda didn't mind the bed rest at first, but she showed signs of getting tired of the whole situation as each day passed. She kept her appointments each week at the hospital with the non-stress tests, which all came back with good results. The whole family was so excited about Christmas and the thought of a new year's baby. As Christmas approached, I sensed Brenda was becoming more stressed. She told me everything was okay, but I had a bad feeling something was going on with her. Suddenly everything started to go wrong.

"On December twenty-first, I was getting ready to leave for

work around 5 a.m. when Brenda walked into the kitchen. I could tell something wasn't right and asked her what was wrong. She said that she had suffered with a bad headache all night and didn't feel well, but she was afraid to take anything until she talked to Doc later in the morning. I asked her if she wanted me to stay home and take her to the doctor, but she resisted and said everything would be fine. I told her to call me if her symptoms changed. I promised her I would call later on in the morning to check on her.

"When I called later, she told me she had just gotten out of the shower and was getting ready to go into the office to get checked. She said that the headache was no better and her vision had begun to blur. Feeling helpless, all I could say was to keep me informed and that I loved her.

"Brenda was moving pretty slow and didn't make it to the office until after lunch. When she walked in the backdoor of the clinic, she could see Doc pulling into the parking lot from his lunch. Doc walked in and asked her what was going on. She told him about the bad headache, blurred vision, and how horrible she was feeling. Doc took her blood pressure, and then he took it again. Brenda's pressure was 160 over 100. He said they would go ahead and get a urine specimen while she was there. The urine specimen showed plus one plus in her urine, which was not good. These were sure signs of superimposed preeclampsia, which were not good for the baby or Brenda. Doc told Brenda to call me at work so I could start heading home because he was sure Dr. Hall was going to want to see her. Doc, as usual, was right. When he called Dr. Hall and told him what was going on with Brenda, Dr. Hall told Doc that it was time to end the pregnancy before her condition declined any further. He said he wanted her to come to the hospital ASAP, prepared to have the baby because he would induce labor as soon as she was admitted.

"After getting the message at work to come home, I had no idea what was going on but figured it was not good. I told my boss there was a possibility I might not be able to work the next few days. After I thought about it, in a few days it would be Christmas. Pulling into the driveway, I could tell Brenda was home by all the lights on in the house. It was only four thirty and it was already getting dark. I had no idea what to expect when I walked in the door, but I was surprised to see Brenda with a big smile on her face. She said she felt like crap, but Dr. Hall said to come prepared to have a baby. She was so ready to get this over. Surprised, I said, 'Now?' She told me to get in the shower because we needed to go now.

"The hospital was a sixty-mile drive. We were like little kids waiting for our big present. I couldn't believe it was time to finally have the baby! On top of that, we were only a few days short of thirty-seven weeks. We were getting close to the hospital when Brenda looked at me and asked if I was hungry. Puzzled, I didn't know the right answer. She said that she needed to eat before we got to the hospital. I asked if the doctor told her to stop off for dinner. With an evil look, she said, 'I'm going to be in labor for God only knows how long, and I want Red Lobster!' Knowing it was probably going to haunt me later, I pulled off the highway and turned towards her favorite place to eat.

"When we finally arrived at the hospital, the nurses treated us like we were late for our own wedding. They immediately started inducing Brenda. I have to admit from that point on I was in uncharted waters as far as labor and delivery go. Even though we had gone through the maternity classes, I was still uncomfortable with the whole situation. As time passed, I started figuring out my role, to do what I was told.

"Brenda had been in labor for three or four hours, but nothing was happening. It was just after midnight when a nurse came into the room and told us she was going to shut Brenda down for the night so she could get some rest."

"Wait, let's stop!" Mr. Stone quickly interrupted. "Why would they stop labor when they just started inducing her? If you left work early because Dr. Hall thought it was time for the baby to be born, why would he start labor and then stop it? This doesn't make sense."

"I know, we didn't understand either. They were in every fifteen minutes checking monitors and Brenda's vitals. We really didn't get much rest because of that." I replied. "I'm sorry if this is taking too much of your time. Do you want me to speed things up?" I asked.

"No, you're doing a fantastic job," Mr. Stone replied. "This is all very interesting. Do you need a break or something to drink?"

I said that I was fine, but I was really thinking how a good stiff drink would taste right about then. That would have had me talking till midnight though.

"Okay, what happened next? How was Brenda feeling at this point?" Mr. Stone asked.

I continued. "December twenty-second started off very early. They started to induce Brenda again just before 6 a.m. Brenda was feeling fine as I remember, we just wanted the whole thing to be over. I know her blood pressure was fine and the fetal monitor was normal because I asked every time they checked. The hours passed slowly. Brenda was having contractions, but nothing would progress. She never dilated past a one. I just sat there and watched TV. I tried to sneak out a few times as lunch time approached, but she stopped me every time. She told me if she couldn't eat or drink, I didn't need to either. She did finally let me get something, but I made it quick.

"As evening approached, Dr. Hall finally showed up making his rounds at the hospital. He followed his normal routine of checking the monitors and charts, then motioned me to follow him into the hall. I met him just outside the room when he told me that everything was stable with Brenda and that he knew Christmas was just over a day away. He said it was against his medical judgment to let Brenda go home for Christmas, but if I promised she would follow strict bed rest and check in every day, that he would let us go home that night. I told him yes.

"Did anyone else hear this conversation between you and Dr. Hall?" asked Mr. Stone.

"No, we were alone," I replied. "Hall walked back in the room and told Brenda that she could go home with strict bed rest. He said, 'If you have any problems, I mean anything, call me.' He wanted us back at the hospital on the twenty-seventh at 6 a.m. so he could induce her again. It was nice being able to go home for Christmas. Gina was really worried and missing her mother. We needed to spend some quality time with her before the twenty-seventh arrived."

Driving home that night, I started thinking about Hall's "against my medical judgment to let you go home for the holiday" speech in the hallway. What the hell did that mean? Should we have stayed at the hospital? Did he think something bad could happen? I was driving myself crazy thinking about it. Everything turned out fine, though. We celebrated Christmas with both sides of the family. I let Brenda rest on the couch instead of in bed. It also gave me a few extra days to plan for the days ahead.

CHAPTER 2

The twenty-seventh of December arrived a little early for me. For some reason I woke up at 1:30 a.m. and couldn't go back to sleep. I knew this was supposed to be the day we had been waiting for, but for some unknown reason something was really bothering me about what was going to happen that day. Ever since Dr. Hall had motioned me out into the hall with his "I'm going to let you go home for Christmas against my medical judgment" speech, I had had a bad feeling. Why did he motion me into the hallway for his little speech instead of talking to Brenda and me in her hospital room? Brenda was his patient, not me. If he had trouble with his medical judgment, she was the first person that should have been told. I didn't say anything to Brenda because she already had enough on her plate. Maybe I was overthinking the whole situation. The doctor had made it clear that we needed to make it to this date. Well the day had arrived. We were at thirty-seven weeks. So many prayers from our family and friends had been passed along to help get us to that point. We were so fortunate.

I was already showered and dressed when the alarm went off at 4 a.m. Brenda spent her time packing a bag for the days ahead while I checked on all our outside animals, making sure they had plenty food and water. This was becoming too much a normal routine for the both of us—up at 4 a.m., arrive at the hospital before 6 a.m. to induce contractions, nothing happens, and then we go home. As we drove to the hospital, something seemed very different this time, though. We were so excited the last time, just before Christmas, driving to the hospital. We even stopped off at Brenda's favorite restaurant to celebrate. The second time seemed more businesslike for some reason. This was the day the doctor had drilled into our minds for months. Was he going to double the Pitocin in Brenda's IV to make it all happen? I could sense it was all going to come to a big climax that day.

I continued telling our story to Mr. Stone. "When we arrived at the hospital, we immediately went to labor and delivery on the third floor of the hospital. In no time, Brenda was hooked up to the monitors and her IV. It wasn't long and she was already beginning to have contractions. As I gazed out the window in her room, the sky started

19

to turn a beautiful red in the east. I remembered my dad always saying 'Red sky morning, sailor's warning' when I was younger. It usually indicated an approaching storm system. Well, he was correct about an approaching storm. We were under a winter storm warning, starting later that day and going into the next. The weather people called for four to eight-plus inches of blowing snow. This added more fuel to my fire. What was Dr. Hall going to do if nothing happened that day? Would he send us home in a winter storm or keep inducing Brenda?

"The hours passed. Brenda only dilated to a one. It was the same story again, just a different day. I sat there and prayed that her labor would start moving along. I could tell she was reaching her breaking point. Her vital signs seemed good. Her blood pressure was okay. Nothing on the fetal monitor indicated any problems, to my knowledge. Watching the news people freak out on TV over the approaching winter storm was keeping me entertained. From my vantage point on the third floor of the hospital, it looked like the storm was already here. It was beginning to snow.

"I finally slipped out to grab a quick bite to eat. When I got back to the room, I could tell something was wrong. Brenda got more and more agitated as each minute passed. I had seen this before, and I knew something was about to happen. She had been in labor over eight hours, and still nothing was happening. Suddenly Brenda hit the nurse's button on her bed. Within a minute, the nurse came into the room and asked what she needed. Brenda said that we wanted to see Dr. Hall as soon as possible. The nurse said he should be there in a few hours."

I watched the snow fall out the window. It was really coming down heavy and starting to accumulate on the streets. I wondered what was going to happen next.

"Dr. Hall arrived at the hospital around 6 p.m. He walked into the room and started checking Brenda's chart and she started unloading her frustrations on him. She said she couldn't take it anymore, and she asked why nothing was happening. He waited until she was completely finished, kind of smiled, and said 'Let's do a C-section.' Brenda and I looked at each other in total shock! Brenda turned back to Dr. Hall and asked when. He said we could do it right now and suggested I go get something to eat while they prepared Brenda for surgery."

Mr. Stone interrupted again and said, "Let's stop here for a moment. He just said 'Let's do a C-section' without any type of explanation?"

"Yes, with a smile on his face," I replied.

"Brenda and the baby were not in any distress?" Mr. Stone asked.

"No, all her vitals seemed fine," I said. "It was like he had planned it all along. I feel bad now for not asking more questions. It just took us by total surprise... It was crazy! Never in a million years did I think that would be his next move. I thought a C-section was a last resort option or in the case of an emergency—"

"I wonder if the doctor was planning a trip out of town and wanted this problem taken care of before he left," Mr. Stone interrupted. "I'm sorry, please continue."

"I went down to the cafeteria to get something to eat," I continued. "I picked out a big hot dog covered with chili and cheese. That was a big mistake. I only ate a few bites. I was filled with so many emotions about what was getting ready happen. Something just didn't seem right about the whole situation. I couldn't figure out why I had such a bad feeling about what was about to happen. Brenda's vital signs had been great all day, and nothing seemed unusual about the welfare of the baby. Why were we jumping the gun and doing a C-section? I went back to the room to check on Brenda. She was all prepped and ready, all we needed was Dr. Hall.

"When he entered the room, it was 7:15 p.m. He asked Brenda if she was ready, and she replied "Yes!" with a smile. Dr. Hall told me I was welcome to join them in the operating room if I liked, but I told him I didn't think that was a very good idea. Everyone laughed as they started wheeling Brenda to surgery. I followed all the way to the operating room. Dr. Hall told Brenda he would see her in a few minutes. I kissed Brenda, told her I loved her, and said good luck. She said, 'I love you!'

"I stood just outside the operating room and leaned against the block wall as they prepared her. I could hear everything going on because the door was still open. Dr. Hall said 'Let's get started.' He

21

was talking the whole time, using medical terminology I could not understand. Suddenly I heard him say, 'Well, Keith is getting the baby boy he wanted.' At the same time a baby started crying. With tears flowing down my face, I leaned back against the wall and said 'Thank you, God, thank you so much!'

"Brett was born at 7:35 p.m. He weighed five pounds two ounces and was nineteen inches long. A nurse came rushing out with him wrapped in a blanket. She said, 'Meet your daddy!' I touched him and said 'Hello!' She quickly started away and told me I could see him through the nursery window. My attention turned back to Brenda. I walked to a small room between the nursery and labor and delivery. They told me Brenda would be brought there after recovery and Dr. Hall would be out to talk with me soon. I waited a few minutes, then thought it might be a good time to call both our parents. I knew everyone was worried since they hadn't heard from us all day. After calling everyone with the great news, I started walking back to wait for Dr. Hall. Walking down the hall, I passed the nursery window and could see Brett. He looked so tiny! I proudly stood for several minutes watching him and all the activity behind the window. I noticed something very unusual about the way Brett was breathing. It looked like he was having a hard time taking in each breath.

"Dr. Hall walked up to me with a strange look on his face. He told me Brenda was doing fine and that she would be out of recovery in about an hour. He said everything went very well, and then he said something very strange to me. He said, 'Everything will be fine, I promise everything is going to be okay.' I thanked him and asked him to keep me informed about Brenda. As Dr. Hall walked away, I began to think about what he had just told me. What the hell was he talking about? Was something wrong that I didn't know about?

"Another person approached me and introduced herself as Doctor Dawson. She was the pediatrician on call that evening. Dr. Dawson immediately told me how concerned she was about Brett's breathing. She said that Brett was very pre-mature. She estimated him to be approximately thirty-two weeks with increased respiratory stress, grunting, and retracting, and it seemed to be getting more pronounced as time passed. She placed him underneath a hood with thirty percent oxygen. Because of Brett's prematurity and the snowstorm outside, she called Children's Memorial Hospital to send a medical team as soon as possible to transfer Brett to their facility. She said they could provide the proper care for him if his condition continued to decrease. The helicopter was grounded because of the storm, so they sent a life support vehicle that Dr. Dawson expected to arrive within the hour. I thanked her and asked that she please do what she could.

"I walked back down the hall and sat down in a chair. I tried to grasp everything that was going on. Things were happening too fast. I had so many different thoughts running through my mind. How could Brett be premature! Dr. Hall said the baby was fully developed. Was that why he told me everything would be fine? What the hell was happening! I asked a nurse if she would find out how Brenda was doing, and she told me Brenda would be coming out of recovery very soon.

"Dr. Dawson walked back into the room and told me she was increasing the oxygen level to fifty percent. I asked about the medical team from Children's Memorial Hospital. She said the winter storm was slowing them down but they would be arriving soon. I started wondering what I was going to do if the medical team arrived and Brenda was still in recovery. If I followed the baby to Children's Memorial, Brenda was going to freak out not knowing what was going on after she came out of recovery. I thought about calling our families, but I didn't want to risk anyone trying to drive in the snow storm. I sat there thinking about what was going on. Maybe I misunderstood the doctor when she said the baby was approximately thirty-two weeks. How could our baby be that premature?

"Around fifteen minutes later they brought Brenda back from recovery. She was still really out of it. She asked about the baby but fell back asleep before I could answer. Slowly, she started to wake up. She started to understand what was going on when another person walked into the room. It was a young lady wearing a uniform that resembled a flight suit. She was part of the medical team sent to transfer Brett. Her name was Kimberly. She explained that the medical team needed to get Brett stabilized before he could be transported. Brenda asked about is his condition, and Kimberly told us that he was very sick because of his breathing problems. They were trying to get

Brett back into an environment that would help stabilize his condition. She told us she needed to get back to Brett and that she would inform us if anything changed.

"Brenda asked me what was going on. All I could tell her was that Brett was premature and having breathing difficulties. I told her everything I knew. Brenda looked at me with a very confused look and asked how he could be premature when she was supposed to be at thirty-seven weeks. I told her that Dr. Dawson thought he was around thirty-two weeks. How could Brett be five weeks premature? A terrible feeling ran through my body. My son was only a few hours old, and there was a chance that he wasn't going to make it through the night. Why was this happening?

"Kimberly returned a few minutes later and told us Brett's condition was deteriorating fast. He was on ninety percent oxygen and still not stabilized. Again she said it was very critical that they get him stabilized and back into a familiar environment, but she warned us that severe breathing difficulties could be harmful to a newborn. If Brett did require one hundred percent oxygen, there was a chance of brain damage, resulting in blindness or other complications. Alarms started sounding from the nursery, and Kimberly yelled that she needed to go.

"By that time Brenda was starting to realize exactly what was happening. I held her hand as we listened to one monitor alarm sound after another. It wasn't just one alarm but several, each with different beeps that were making us crazy. We could hear voices working as each alarm sounded. We were both so helpless!

"Suddenly everything went silent. You could hear a pin drop. Brenda and I looked at each other, fearing the worst. Several minutes passed before Kimberly walked back into the room. She told us that Brett had weakened to the point where he could not breathe on his own. They had to place him on a ventilator with one hundred percent oxygen, but they had him stabilized enough for transport. Kimberly said they needed to get him to doctors that were experienced with that situation because his condition was very serious. She told us they would bring Brett down shortly so Brenda could say goodbye, but I needed to meet them at the hospital to register him.

"All I could do was hold on to Brenda. I'm sure the same thoughts and prayers were running through her mind as we waited silently. A short time later, the medical team rolled Brett into the room. He was naked, flat on his back, with tubes going into his mouth and nose. You could hear the sound of the ventilator making him breathe. Wires were attached to his head and several other parts of his body, along with IV's pumping fluids into his system. The incubator he was placed in was providing the environment keeping him stable. Kimberly told us that we could touch him through the hole in the side glass. Brenda became overwhelmed with emotions as she caressed his tiny body. We were both in tears as they wheeled him away. I kissed Brenda and told her I needed to go. Brenda pleaded with me to keep her informed about his condition. I promised I would.

"Our car was covered with at least six inches of snow when I walked out to the parking lot. After starting the engine, I couldn't find the brush or scraper to clean the snow off. I ended up using my bare hands. I could see the life support vehicle leaving with Brett. They were not using their lights or sirens, so I figured that was a good sign. Driving to Children's Memorial Hospital on a good day is usually a thirty-minute drive. That night was not a good night to be driving. It was 2:30 a.m. when I got on the highway. Snow was still coming down heavy, and the road was completely snow packed. Apparently I was the only one traveling at that time. I had the whole highway to myself.

"After arriving at Children's Memorial, I walked into the emergency entrance and they directed me to admitting and registration. When finished in admitting, I was told that Brett was on the second floor in the neonatal intensive care unit. I was instructed to go to the waiting area just outside the doors of the unit and wait for the doctor. It was 3:45 a.m., and the halls and the waiting area were very dark. I could see someone sleeping on a sofa in the corner. I paced back and forth in the dark hallway, waiting to hear something. I had been awake over twenty-four hours at that point. The stress of all the events that morning and the day before were starting to drag me down. I needed some coffee or something with caffeine to wake me up.

By 5 a.m. I still hadn't talked with or seen anyone except for the person still asleep on the sofa. I was beginning to wonder if I was at the correct waiting area. At five fifteen the double doors popped open. A guy walked out towards me. He wasn't wearing the typical white coat and stethoscope around his neck, so I didn't figure him to be a doctor. He walked up asked if I was Baby Brett's dad. I said I was and asked if he could tell me how Brett was doing. He said Brett was a very challenging case because he was several weeks premature. I said 'What? I was told Brett was full term, or, I'm sorry, thirty-seven weeks!' The doctor again said that Brett was approximately thirty-two to thirty-three weeks and that he was presenting symptoms of hyaline membrane disease with questionable persistent fetal circulation."

Mr. Stone stopped me and asked, "How did the doctor know your son was only at thirty-two to thirty-three weeks?"

"I don't know! By that time I was so confused about everything being explained to me concerning dates, weeks, symptoms. I told the doctor to please explain what was going on in normal terms that I could understand. He said, 'Your son is in respiratory distress.' He explained that hyaline membrane disease is a respiratory disease of the newborn, especially the premature infant, in which a membrane composed of proteins and dead cells line the tiny air sacs in the lung, making gas exchange difficult or impossible. It also can be called respiratory distress syndrome. Respiratory distress syndrome almost always occurs in newborns born before thirty-seven weeks of gestation. The more premature the baby is, the greater is the chance of developing respiratory distress syndrome.

"The doctor continued to explain what they were doing to stabilize Brett's condition. He realized that his words were going in one ear and out the other. The doctor said he would keep me informed regarding any changes in Brett's condition, but I should be prepared because his condition could decrease in the next twenty-four to forty-eight hours. He gave me a number to call anytime that put me in direct contact with his nurse. Then he told me to check on Brenda and get some rest. I asked if I would be able to see him, and the doctor said I could visit Brett as often as I wanted. Right then they needed to get him stabilized, and I needed to go to Brenda, and both of us needed to get some rest. He promised they would notify me if Brett's condition changed.

"Walking out of the hospital, I noticed the snow had pretty well let up. I started the car and just sat there being too tired to clean the snow off the outside. I didn't know what to do. Should I stay with my newborn son or go check on my wife? I figured Brenda was probably going crazy not knowing how Brett was doing. I started back to check on her and fill her in on what was going on. The roads were a mess, so I didn't make it back to the hospital until 8 a.m.

"Mr. Stone, that is pretty much the whole story," I said. "A few other things happened concerning the doctor, but I've already taken enough of your time."

"No," said Mr. Stone, "please tell me everything. Did Brett's condition improve?"

"No, his condition declined even further. The next day Brett's lungs collapsed, and they had to put in chest tubes. He was still not breathing on his own and was still on one hundred percent oxygen. The doctor ordered ultrasounds and CT scans of his head because he suspected seizure activity. When I visited him, I would have to scrub in and put on a gown and mask. Brett was the biggest baby in the care unit, as far as I could tell. It was an amazing sight looking at all the premature infants. Most of them were much smaller than Brett, probably weighing only two or three pounds. All I could do was stand and watch Brett lie so helplessly. A few times he opened his eyes and started crying, but sadly his cry produced no sound because of the tubes running through his mouth and nose.

"On Day Three, the hospital gave Brenda a pass to visit Brett for a few hours. She was doing great after the C-section and was hoping to get released for home the next day. Brett's condition was about the same, with no major problems like the previous days. Brett's nurse informed me that the financial office needed to talk with me and that the business offices were in the basement of the hospital. I told Brenda to spend time with Brett while I went down to see what they wanted.

"The financial office was a very small, dark, and cluttered room. The gentleman that greeted me offered me a chair. He fumbled through a stack of papers, then looked up at me and said that, as of midnight that night, the total expenses on our account would be in excess of twenty-six thousand dollars. I just sat there for a second. I figured the costs were piling up with all the care our son was receiving. Shocked and overwhelmed over this amount, I asked him to please send an itemized bill to my medical provider and then bill me the difference. I promised I would pay back every penny, even if it took the rest of my life."

Mr. Stone asked, "Have you paid the hospital balance off?"

"No, our balance is still around six thousand dollars," I replied. "I have never missed a payment, though, and will someday get the whole balance paid off! We have paid off all the other medical bills."

"You mentioned a few other things happened that were unusual," Mr. Stone prompted.

I said, "Yes, one of the days when I was traveling back and forth between Brenda and Brett, something unusual did happen. I was walking through the lobby of the hospital towards the elevator to go up and see Brenda when I ran into the nurse who put on the prenatal classes we attended. She seemed like she remembered me and asked how I did in delivery. When I told her about the C-section and all the problems after, she seemed to become angry. She asked who our doctor was, and when I told her she stormed off.

"Another instance is when I got on the elevator to go up and see Brenda one night. The door opened at one of the floors and Dr. Hall got on the elevator. He asked how Brett was doing and if there was anything we needed. I told him Brett was stable but still not breathing on his own. He then told me that if I needed a place to stay, anytime, that I could stay at his home. I thanked him for his generosity, but declined. When I told Brenda about this, she just raved about how nice he was. For some reason, I thought it was a little unusual.

"Brenda was discharged from the hospital on New Year's Eve. It was great to sleep in our own bed again. Brett's condition seemed to have hit rock bottom, and he was starting to show very slight signs of improving. We called the 800-number three or four times a day to check on his condition. Late in the evening on New Year's Day we contacted the nurse to check on Brett. We were given fantastic news. Brett had been taken off the ventilator and was now breathing on his own! He was still on eighty percent oxygen, but he was showing great signs of improving. Brenda and I celebrated the great news with a few cocktails.

In the next few days, Brett made dramatic improvement. We started spending more and more time with him as he started to recover. On January ninth, he was transferred back to the hospital where he was born. Since Brett was fed intravenously for so many days, he lost the instinct to feed on his own. He needed to learn how to suck on a bottle of formula because Brenda was past the point of being able to breastfeed him. The hospital wanted Brett to reach his original birth weight before they would release him. Five days later we were allowed to take our son home for the first time.

"At first we were very protective with Brett. We allowed immediate family to come visit only if they were healthy. As time passed and Brett gained weight, we started to let our guard down with our restrictions. Within weeks our life seemed to be getting back to normal. Brett was doing great. He was such a cute baby! We were so happy after taking Brett back for his follow-up appointments to test for any complications arising from his prematurity. They told us he was doing great."

CHAPTER 3

"I finally got a call to go back to work after being laid off for several weeks and Brenda was making the arrangements to do the same. Brett was going to stay with the same lady who watched Gina when she was a baby. Everything was going great as we passed Valentine's Day and approached Easter. We visited Brenda's sister Donna and her husband Rob towards the end of March. They lived about four hours south of our location. This was our first trip as a family with Brett. He was very fussy the entire time. The days and weeks ahead were the same. Was it colic? After spending Easter weekend in the hospital for tests, it was determined that he might be allergic to the formula we were feeding him. I think this was about the time Brenda started to realize something was seriously wrong with our son. I don't know if a doctor or nurse told her something during that weekend or if she figured it out for herself. She was keeping a baby's first year calendar of memories, and after this date there were never any more entries.

"Spring turned into summer. Brett was crawling everywhere through our house. He would go from room to room in a blink of an eye. We got the biggest kick out of him following us through the house. He would crawl military-style from his room, through the dining room, and into the living room. We laughed at him because he would get in front of us, look up at the ceiling fan, and giggle. It was so funny!

"Brenda took Brett for his checkup in August with his pediatrician, Dr. Dawson. During the examination, Brenda told her about how he was making us laugh at home. Dr. Dawson asked how long he had been doing this, and Brenda said probably for the last month. Dr. Dawson then asked, 'When he looks up at the ceiling, does he keep on doing it?'

"Brenda replied, 'Two, three times, maybe more. I never thought about it, why do you ask?'

"Dr. Dawson looked at Brett, then turned back to Benda, and said, 'I want you to get Brett to Children's Memorial Hospital as soon as possible to see a pediatric neurologist for tests. I believe what you're seeing are actually infantile spasms. I'm not sure about this, but we need to rule it out quickly.'"

Infantile spasms is a rare seizure disorder of infancy and early childhood. The onset is predominantly in the first year of life. Infantile spasms is listed as a rare disease and affects less than two hundred thousand people in the US population. Some of the possible long-term effects can be difficult for any parent or caregiver to face. Children with infantile spasms are at risk of developing a range of cognitive and developmental problems. Some may have difficulty learning basic movements—such as sitting up, crawling, and reaching—or reaching certain milestones as quickly as most children. Delay in effective treatment can also reduce the likelihood of the child doing well developmentally.

"It's so sad. Something we thought was so cute was actually doing serious harm to our son, and we didn't even know it. A simple eye deviation, looking up, was actually a sign of a serious brain injury. The weeks and months after that are hard to describe. I remember us admitting Brett into the hospital in August for tests. They were monitoring him while they tried different medications to control the infantile spasms.

"Brenda and I never left Brett by himself while he was hospitalized. We were able to work it out somehow, juggling our work schedules. When we took Brett home, it was like we had lost our son. He seemed so drugged up. The infantile spasms had stopped but we had lost our son in the process.

"Mr. Stone, I'm sorry, this is very hard to talk about," I said. "I have one more thing for you. I think it was the six-week check-up Brenda had with Dr. Hall after giving birth. During the office visit he asked how things were going. Brenda told him that Brett was doing great, but because of the bad weather I was still laid off from work. He asked Brenda if we needed money to help get by for the time being. Brenda declined his generosity of course and told him we would be fine.

"A couple of weeks later he called Brenda at the office. He told her the hospital was doing an investigation on him regarding the amount of C-sections he had performed in the previous months.

He asked Brenda if she could get Doc to write a letter to the hospital backing his decisions," I explained as I handed him a copy of the typed letter from Dr. Russell, dated April ninth.

Dr. Russell stated that the pregnancy went well until early November, when problems started occurring. He mentioned that these included decreased movement of the fetus, protein in Brenda's urine, and increased blood pressure. In December, he explained that she started going for non-stress tests. He wrote, in part, "On December twenty-first I checked her, and it felt like the head had dropped. She had protein in her urine, her blood pressure had increased excessively, and she was having severe headaches. After I consulted with Dr. Hall about her condition, she was admitted to the hospital. After reviewing the situation, I totally agree with the action that Dr. Hall took."

"Mr. Stone, thank you for taking the time to meet with me," I said. "This is all I remember. Do you think this is worth investigating any further?"

"Yes, I do," Mr. Stone said. "The statute of limitations have passed regarding claims that you have as parents, but the limitations regarding your son extend until he is twenty-one years old. This will be a very lengthy process, though. I will need your permission as parents to enter into the following contingent fee agreement with my law firm:

> RE: Premature birth of Brett J. Meyer by C-section resulting in oxygen induced injuries and cerebral palsy. All possibly due to negligence of Dr. Robert Hall in misjudging length of gestation and doing unnecessary C-section and possibly due to negligent administering of oxygen by St. Joseph's Hospital and Children's Memorial Hospital.

"Please do not involve Dr. Russell in any way regarding this investigation," I asked. "I know Brenda will not sign off on this if he is involved. He does not know anything about what we are doing."

Mr. Stone said, "I will need copies of Brenda and Brett's records. Can she get me those records?"

"Brenda will send you anything you need."

"Do you have any questions regarding the contingent fee agreement?" Mr. Stone asked.

"Yes, this paragraph about costs and expenses. How much do you think this will cost us per month? We are not in a position right now to take on any more bills."

Mr. Stone said, "Keith, let's not get concerned with costs at this point. I have over twenty years' trial experience in medical and personal injury cases. A case like this can take several years before it is settled or goes to trial. Let me assure you that if I feel we do not have enough proof of malpractice in this case, it will be discontinued. Let me write this into the agreement." He crossed out the word "monthly" in the sentence regarding payment arrangements and signed with his initials. He then added the following sentence: "Attorneys will wait until resolution of lawsuit or until claim is discontinued to arrange for collection of costs." He also put his initials next to this sentence.

"Do you have any more questions?" he asked.

"No, I think you have answered everything. Thank you so much!"

"All I need is for you and Brenda to sign and date this agreement and return it as soon as possible," Mr. Stone said. "Please call me anytime if you have any further questions. It's been a pleasure talking with you."

Living in a rural community, we were very skeptical to let anyone know about the investigation we started. We told our parents and close family, of course. What about Dr. Russell? He needed to be told before red flags started going up. Brenda called Doc a few nights later and asked if we could come by to talk. We told Doc everything. Brenda told him she was afraid this could jeopardize her working relationship with him. He supported our decision but warned us that proving negligence would be very difficult.

Time started to pass very quickly. Communication from the Stone Law Firm consisted of a monthly statement that showed very little activity regarding our case. Gathering medical records was the only thing happening at that point. Weeks turned to months. Finally I called Mr. Stone's office in the early days of March. It had been almost a year since I met with him about our situation. Brett was four years old. Mr. Stone told me they were still processing all the records.

"Your case is very interesting," he said. "It's very difficult to find someone with the medical knowledge who will read these records and give a different opinion regarding another doctor. We are working very hard on your case. This is all I can tell you at this point."

We were very disappointed that Mr. Stone didn't have more encouraging news for us. I started to wonder if we would ever find out what caused Brett's disability.

Our lives began to focus on both of our growing children. Gina was nine years old. She loved playing and helping out with her little brother. Gina would spend hours with Brett playing video games. Sometimes he would just watch her play, learning the secrets and shortcuts on how to proceed through the games. We knew then that he could see and follow objects with his vision. Our only problem was trying to figure out what. He would lay flat on his back, looking back at the TV, playing the video games. He actually did pretty well playing that way.

Brett was crawling everywhere throughout the house very quickly but not showing any signs of walking. Brenda was working her full-time job, getting Gina up and off to school every day, dressing, feeding, and grooming Brett, and dropping him off at the sitter. The company that I worked for landed a major contract to totally renovate the world headquarters location of a major corporation in the city. For the next eleven months, I was going to be working seven days a week, ten to twelve hours a day. I was fortunate to be working. Commercial building had been very slow for several years. We started paying off many of the medical bills with all the overtime I was working. My day consisted of getting up and leaving home by 4:30 a.m., driving seventy miles to my job, working twelve hours, and heading back home to do it over again.

One weekend I was lucky enough to come home early from work. Brenda talked me into going to a disability expo that was going on at the convention center in town. I never thought about how fast Brett was growing. It was normal procedure to pick Brett up off the floor, put him in the car seat until we arrived at our destination, then carry him in and put him back on the floor. We did have a stroller for shopping and other activities, but Brett was growing out of it fast. This was the last thing I would have ever thought about at that point, but it was starting to become a real problem for Brenda. All the lifting was beginning to hurt her back.

Going to the disability expo was an eye-opening experience for me, looking at all the equipment and medical aids. Of course a great sales person saw me carrying my four-year-old son through the exhibits. He motioned me over. He said, "You look like you need a break, Dad. Put your son in this chair!" It was a small wheelchair. As soon as Brett was seated in the chair, the salesman's hands started moving as fast as he could talk. He was making different adjustments to the chair, making Brett as comfortable and sitting as properly as possible. I was amazed how good he looked in the chair, or wheelchair. This was the first step in realizing my son had a disability. The wheelchair cost around nine thousand dollars. If we were lucky, the chair would probably last two years before Brett outgrew it. Our medical provider would have to approve the cost of the chair. The salesperson was confident enough that it would be approved and let Brett leave in the wheelchair.

Our next obstacle was to find a vehicle that would fit our situation. All the cars we owned at that point were four-door sedans. Brenda had to bend down to put Brett into and out of a car seat. A wheelchair had to be figured into the lifting process. Our next big purchase was a minivan. It was our first new vehicle. We were so proud of our purchase. Instead of bending down to put Brett into a car seat, all Brenda had to do was lift him into a captain chair. It was so much easier. The wheelchair was very small and lightweight. It fit perfectly in the rear of the van.

I asked my boss if I could take off one weekend. We wanted to take our new purchase on a short trip for the first time to visit Brenda's sister. Brenda's mom and dad were going to keep the kids. We were so excited to get away for a weekend and spend time with Donna and Rob and our two little nieces. We didn't arrive at their home until Friday evening. They had the perfect home for visiting family and friends. The main part of the house was divided by a breezeway that led to a bi-level recreation area. The entertainment area was down, and the loft was a sleeping area. It was perfect! We spent most of our time just visiting with each other.

Saturday night Rob and Donna had a sitter lined up for their girls. We went out to eat and also visited many of the local establishments for drinks. Of course I insisted we go in our new van. It was a great evening. On the way back late that night, Brenda's sister asked me to pull over because she was going to be sick. When Rob opened the sliding door for Donna, she kind of took a few steps and rolled into the ditch. Brenda and I laughed as Rob helped her back to the van. She wanted to sit up front, so Rob moved back with Brenda. I drove a few more miles when Donna said it was getting too hot in the van and she needed air. I rolled down both front windows... It was twenty degrees outside. Donna's next move was almost predictable. A steady flow of projectile vomit went straight from her mouth directly into the defroster vents on the dashboard. In one split second our new-car smell was gone. Brenda and I still laugh about that night. The next day it was time to head home and get back to reality.

Orthopedic problems soon became our major concern. Brett started seeing Dr. Williams at the orthopedic clinics. Dr. Williams thought it was time for Brett to start seeing the world in a different way—on his feet. He said, "Brett will never be able to walk down the street, but I think he will be able to walk with the assistance of a walker and specially designed braces. Before we can start this process though, Brett will require surgery and an enormous amount of physical therapy." We were so excited that Brett might be able to walk someday.

The surgery Dr. Williams planned to perform was called bilateral posterior tibial tendon repair, spring ligament plication, and peroneal tendon lengthening to correct bilateral planovalgus feet. It involved incisions on both sides of each ankle to lengthen and tighten tendons and ligaments to balance the foot for walking. At first I was terrified to let someone cut my son, but then I knew we had to do everything possible to give Brett a chance to walk. This was the first of several major surgeries Brett would have to endure in his lifetime. It really doesn't matter if it's the first or the fifth surgery, watching your child being wheeled off to surgery is very emotional. That first surgery went very well, or as Dr. Williams told us, "Perfect."

When Brett came out of recovery, he was really out of it. He was sleeping in a fetal position and seemed very comfortable. He had casts on both feet that extended up to each knee. Around 8 p.m. I told Brenda I was going home to get ready for work the next day. I said I'd be back the next day after work and to call if something changed. Brenda said her mom was coming early in the morning and that she'd be fine.

The next day went great for me. I stopped off at home to clean up after work before going to the hospital. After a quick shower, I called Brett's room to see if Brenda needed anything from home. Brenda said, "Please get up here! I've had a horrible day!" When I asked what was wrong, Brenda replied, "Brett has been screaming in pain all day! Please get up here!" I could hear Brett crying in the background.

"Why didn't you call me?" I asked.

She said, "Just get up here, I can't take it much longer!"

When I arrived at Brett's room, Brenda was a wreck. She said, "Thank God my mother was here to help!" I looked at Vicky, and she gave a smile. I asked Brenda what the hell was going on, and she motioned me towards the hall.

"Brett has been screaming since early this morning," she said. "They told me it was normal after such a surgery. Mom finally got him out of bed and rocked him in the rocking chair. She noticed both casts were pinching into the backs of his legs. I guess when he came out of surgery and went to recovery, Brett went into a fetal position and caused the wet plaster to pinch the circulation in the back of both legs. Dr. Williams has been called and is on his way to cut the casts and relieve the problem."

Dr. Williams walked in with his whole crew, which included students, residents, and interns. We all stood around Brett's bed. One of Dr. Williams understudies explained that he needed to trim the back of the casts to relieve the circulation problem that was causing the pain. It seemed like a simple fix. Anyone that has ever had a broken bone has listened to the same speech. "This saw cannot hurt you!"

We all listened to the young doctor explain the process to

Brett before he started the saw. Brett watched with wide eyes as the doctor placed the saw against the back of his hand to demonstrate that no harm could come from the device. Suddenly blood started flowing from the back of the young doctor's hand. Everyone around the bed looked on amazed at the sight of what happened. I was standing close enough to hear Dr. Williams say, "Idiot!" Brett started screaming, "No, I don't want that! Please, not me!"

Dr. Williams had no choice but take charge of the situation. He told the young intern to leave and get his hand taken care of. He then started talking to Brett, making a joke of what happened. After regaining Brett's confidence, Dr. Williams was able to trim both casts, relieving the pressure causing the pain. We brought Brett home the next day. Within days he was crawling everywhere through the house, banging the casts on everything in his way.

Physical therapy would be our next challenge. When the casts came off weeks later, Dr. Williams was very happy with the results. It was time to get Brett on his feet. Brenda went crazy trying to find a physical therapist in our area that could provide the proper services for Brett's needs. The closest location was at least thirty miles from our home. Douglas County, about twenty-five minutes east of our home, had a preschool program that provided special education to disabled children, including all the related services—physical therapy, occupational therapy, speech therapy, and transportation.

I was amazed when Brenda told me our school district did have a preschool program. The only problem was that they did not provide those services to children with special needs, nor any of the related services like the other school district. Brenda was able to get Brett into the preschool program in the Douglas County district, but we would be responsible to pay for transportation. Since this was our only option, we had no choice but agree to the terms.

Brett started to thrive in the new program. He enjoyed the long ride to school and all the other services being provided to him. We were very impressed by all the feedback we started receiving from the PT, OT, and speech therapist. I started reading the booklets that were being sent home with Brett regarding the education of special needs children. My interest in this information turned into a passion. I started calling different services and organizations regarding our rights during my free time at work. I consulted with different advocacy services about sending our son to another school district for services our district was not providing. My one-hour-plus commute back and forth to work became the perfect time to form a strategy to approach our school district concerning the services they were failing to provide to our son.

One day I arrived home early from work because of bad weather. I called Brenda at work to let her know I was home. She told me this was a great time to confront the school district with my questions. I called the main office to find out who was in charge of special education for the school district. The Director of Special Education, Ms. Fuller, was actually the principal of our daughter's elementary school. Since Gina's school was only a short drive from our house, I quickly showered and drove down to the school, hoping to catch up with Ms. Fuller.

Walking into the small school building, I wondered if I was prepared for this meeting. When I walked up to the secretary and told her my name, she seemed confused. In a small town everyone knows everyone, but, like usual, she didn't recognize me. I quickly told her that my wife was Brenda and our daughter was Gina. She said, "Oh, your Brenda's husband! What do you need?"

"Is Ms. Fuller available to answer some questions?" I asked.

The secretary said she needed to check. She walked into the adjoining office and quickly returned with Ms. Fuller following. She greeted me with a handshake and invited me into her office.

"How can I help you, Mr. Meyer?" she asked.

"I have several questions regarding the preschool program the district provides for children four years of age," I began. "Our son Brett is four years old and was diagnosed with cerebral palsy. We were told that the district does not provide preschool services to special needs children. Why?"

"Mr. Meyer, I'm not familiar with specifics regarding your son," she said. "The preschool program we provide is not structured to handle the needs that your son requires. We do have a program that starts at the kindergarten level that will start addressing his needs."

39

"Why are other districts around our county required to provide special need services to their preschool children?" I asked.

"I'm not familiar with how the other districts around our area handle their preschool programs. Each district can provide different services," she responded. "I just moved here from Nebraska. I'm very familiar with the laws in Nebraska. I'm still not up to speed with this state's regulations."

I thought to myself, how could she have the job title "Director of Special Education" if she wasn't familiar with all the laws and regulations? Was she putting up a smokescreen? She seemed to be very defensive.

After I asked the next question, I realized we were in for a tough fight. I asked, "Why is the school district not required to follow federal law that states every child is entitled to a free and appropriate education? If the district provides a preschool program to normal children, then they also have to provide the same services to special needs children, along with any other related services that child may require, such as physical therapy, occupational therapy, speech therapy, or transportation. If the school district cannot provide these services, they are required to contract for these services with another district."

Ms. Fuller replied, "Mr. Meyer, the school district is not required to follow federal law. We follow state laws and regulations."

I couldn't believe she said that. The school district was not required to follow federal law!

"We will have a program for your son next year," she continued. "I will talk to the superintendent of schools and express your concerns regarding your son. If something different can be done, I will contact you. I'm sorry I couldn't be of more help to you today."

"I'm also sorry we couldn't work this out," I replied. "Please tell the superintendent that if we do not hear anything back regarding our complaints in the next week, we will have no choice but to file due process against the school district. Brenda and I will also be calling our school board representatives with our complaints. Thank you for taking the time to talk with me."

Three days later we received a call from Ms. Fuller. She told Brenda the school district was going to work out preschool services with the Douglas County District. She also said the district would reimburse us for all past and future transportation costs.

This was the first of many confrontations we would have regarding Brett's education. It was a great learning experience, advocating for my son.

CHAPTER 4

When Brett was just over seven years old, we put our house and property on the market to sell. Brenda and I had talked about it for a long time. The market for selling homes was good, and we hoped to move into the small town where Brenda worked. This would give Brett a better chance to be around more people. Gina also liked the idea because she would be close to all her friends. Brenda wanted to be closer to her parents. I just wanted a maintenance-free home that didn't have five hours of grass cutting.

It had been over a year since our last conversation with Mr. Stone. One day that spring I came home a little early from work because of rain. Brenda was home also because the medical office was closed on Thursdays. We both were having a bad day for some reason. I'm sure it was due to something involving the kids, school, or just life in general. After pouring our emotions out on each other and drinking a few drinks, I told Brenda I was going to call Stone. I couldn't believe it had been four years and nothing had happened.

When I called his office, the receptionist put me right through to his office. "Keith, how are you?" he asked. "Is everyone well?"

"Everyone is great, Mr. Stone," I replied. "Brenda and I were wondering if you had anything new to share with us. It's been a long time since our last conversation."

Mr. Stone said he had nothing new to tell us. "We have hit a rock wall concerning your case. Most cerebral palsy cases involve the doctor waiting too long before ending the pregnancy. In your case, the doctor took the baby early, and the records show he did an emergency C-section on Brenda. Until we can find out what caused the cerebral palsy, we have no case."

"Mr. Stone," I quickly responded. "I don't think you're looking at what happened to Brett the same way as we are. It was not an emergency C-section. When we questioned Dr. Hall about the snowstorm that night and our other concerns, he just said 'Let's do a C-section.' There was no emergency! Our question has always been if Brett had been allowed to go full term would he have been normal?"

"You're right," said Mr. Stone. "I never thought about it that way. So you're saying if Hall would have allowed the pregnancy to proceed...another day, a week, or even longer, the circumstances might have changed."

I said, "Yes! If the C-section was an emergency, why would he tell me to go get a bite to eat while they prepared Brenda? If Brenda or Brett were in distress, I would never left her side to get something to eat."

"What you're telling me makes sense," he replied. "I really never looked at the situation that way. I'm going to make some calls. I think it's about time to find someone to read and evaluate the records we have gathered. You will be hearing back from me soon. Please give your family my best regards."

It's amazing how timing can be everything. Brenda and I were having a very bad day. Both of us, for some reason, arrived home early and talked about our problems. I decided to call our attorney, hoping to hear something encouraging after four years. Our attorney seemed to be having a bad day also. We talked for a few minutes when suddenly something I said would change everything and create an explosion of activity.

We received a letter from Ms. Dunkin, an associate with the Stone Law Firm. She stated that Brett's medical records were being reviewed at our request by a medical doctor regarding the issue of medical negligence. This doctor had requested a copy of Brett's latest CT scan and the latest general evaluation of his condition. We needed to call and tell the firm where to send the medical authorizations to obtain these records.

Four days later another legal envelope arrived from Mr. Stone's office with a handwritten note from Ms. Dunkin.

Mr. & Mrs. Meyer:

I enclosed the report from Dr. Darren Allen, the medical expert reviewing Brett's records. Although the doctor has found breaches in the standard of care, he has NOT committed himself on causation. He wants to see additional medical records and Mrs. Meyer is to

43

send me the records we talked about. Before a lawsuit can be merited we need Dr. Allen to substantiate the breaches of care that caused or contributed to cause Brett's medical problems. Please call if you have questions.

Dr. Allen, from north central Florida, had been carefully reviewing the medical records. His opinion would either make or break our case of medical negligence. The following is a letter from Dr. Allen with a summary of his findings:

Dear Mr. Stone:

I reviewed the records sent on this case and find evidence of substandard care that is significant enough, in my opinion, to warrant proceeding with your case. Before discussing the medical issues, however, I would point out some document dates that are interesting, to say the least, and which indicate the induction/delivery was part of a preconceived plan that was not part of emergency management, as claimed by the delivering doctor.

1. The history and physical for the admission where delivery occurred was dictated about a week before attempted induction. NOTE THAT ADMISSION WAS 12/27/83 AT 0600. In other words, no true emergency. Dr. Hall reiterates this elective admission status in the last four lines of the first paragraph of the dictated and typed C-section operative note. He attempts to cover this in the handwritten "Addendum to History" of 12/29/83 after it is apparent this child was having problems.

2. The Discharge Summary was dictated April 3, 1984 after the child had problems. It too states elective induction but seeks to invoke "fetal indications" as the rationale. JCAHO and most hospital rules require these summaries to be done within 14 days of discharge. This breech, by itself, is not substantive but demonstrates the attempts to sanitize the records.

This case asks about the standard of care in 1983 for a patient with chronic hypertension, and asks whether or not there was superimposed toxemia, intrauterine growth retardation or other sign of fetal jeopardy that demanded early delivery.

By past medical history, it is known that this patient had chronic hypertension and was at risk for adverse pregnancy outcome. In the main, these adverse outcomes include teratologic effects of the antihypertensive medication, placental abruption, placental insufficiency, intrauterine growth retardation and superimposed toxemia. Of course, any text can come up with more in a laundry list, but these are the main items. The situation of chronic hypertensive patients becoming pregnant occurs with some frequency and anyone dealing with pregnant patients should be aware of these potential complications and their avoidance and/or management, to at the very least, the nearest referral center.

In this case the attending, Dr. Hall, elected to treat this patient in conjunction with another physician, perhaps an internist. This decision is okay if the principles of obstetric care were followed. They were not.

The drug for choice for these patients is Hydralazine. The physicians here attempted to change Mrs. Meyers to this medication but, due to her headaches during those attempts, they were abandoned. Headache can be due to many things, especially in pregnancy. In an hypertensive, headache can also be due to hypertension. I find no documented hypertension during the attempts to switch nor do not find that this patient was hospitalized for evaluation, medication change, weight control or any reason other than induction attempts during this pregnancy. Proper care would have dictated that the patient be closely observed in the office or hospitalized and switched to Hydralazine. The standard of care is to at least see the patient several times a week during the attempt to change from Corgard to Hydralazine. The records I have do not show that this was done. This error is of little moment since Corgard has been used safely in pregnancy and, as in this case, caused no teratogenic changes and no placental insufficiency.

Placental abruption did not occur and will not be discussed.

The following items will be considered:

Placental insufficiency:

Placental insufficiency is an occurrence where, due to placental changes such as fibrosis, infarct, small size or in its microscopic structure or biochemical function, it is inadequate to transfer waste from the fetus or oxygen and nutrition to it. This situation occurs in chronic hypertensive's and post-dates pregnancy and becomes significant if the effects on the fetus become clinically obvious. In this case, the only placental finding was "prematurity."

Gestational Age:

In order to measure growth or assess growth retardation in the third trimester by ultrasound, a baseline fetal growth curve must be established. In order to consider early delivery because of hypertensive complications, a true due date needs to be established. Due date is established by history of past periods and coitus, the clinical criteria of date of first hearing the fetal heartbeat by stethoscope (18-20 weeks), date of first quickening (feeling the baby move, usual for a first mother at 18 weeks) and by ultrasound. Ultrasound is most accurate in the mid-trimester. In this case, there was no recordation of the interval between periods just before conception. To not get this information is below the standard of care (SOC) and is important because ovulation is 2 weeks before the onset of the next period. If the usual interval for this patient was 5 weeks, her due date would be a week later by these calculations than would be a patient who had 4 week intervals.

Ultrasound in the second trimester is accurate within a week. In this case, most criteria for gestational age ran a week behind the expected and this, along with the delay in quickening, should have prompted the attending to consider the true due date as at least a week later than previously thought. In any event, it should have put him on notice that there might be an inaccurate due date. This should have helped prevent the un-indicated and early attempts to deliver seen here. The standard of care under the clinical circumstances of this case, especially since the past hypertension was known and actual due date could become critical, was to do serial sonograms to plot the growth curve of the baby and carefully document each developmental landmark of the fetus. In addition, fundal size correlates rather well with gestational age in the mid-trimester and can be used as a guide to where one is. If there was an established curve and the baby grew slower than expected, there would have been reason to be concerned and to look at the delivery option due to placental insufficiency. In this case that was not done due to a breach in the standard of care.

In a patient such as this the standard of care is to begin more intensive surveillance of the fetus and mother at 34-36 weeks gestation with the goals of maintaining health of both patients and prolonging the pregnancy as much as possible, consistent with safety. In the third trimester, the main dangers are abruption and placental insufficiency. Abruption did not occur. Placental insufficiency should be sought and can be detected by the use of several standard techniques available in 1983. If found, its effects can be treated with bed rest, nutrition and only under a narrow set of circumstances, not present in this case. The "Biophysical Profile" was quite new and will not be considered as a standard.

Useful terms:

1.   Non-stress test:

This is a test of fetal well being that depends on the integrity of the fetal neurological system. When normal, it shows an acceleration of fetal heart rate after fetal movement. When the NST is reactive it is extremely rare to lose a fetus in the ensuing week due to placental failure, the major danger dealt with in this case. The standard of care in 1983 under these circumstances was to do this test at least weekly and most did it twice a week until delivery. If this test was non-reactive, it could indicate fetal compromise and the test must be followed up. In this case, it was followed up.

2.   Contraction Stress Test:

This is one of the follow up tests if the non-stress test is non-reactive. In 1983 there were several endocrine tests being touted but none became great and none were the standard of care. In the contraction stress test the fetus was stressed by through oxytocin induced uterine contractions. If this test was reactive, it was felt that the fetus was in good health and would remain so for the following week. In this case, the CST showed fetal well being and gave no indication that delivery was indicated.

3.   Fetal Kick Count:

The preceding two tests require medical equipment and personnel. Fetal activity as perceived by the mother is an important indicator of fetal well being for the times between medical visits. If a baby shows a change in its movement pattern, or if there is decreased movement, the patient is to report it to the physician who will then do a non-stress test. In this case the standard of care was followed.

4.   Serial Ultrasound:

A fetus under the effects of placental insufficiency (as is typical for hypertensive patients) will show evidence of this on weekly ultrasound. These should be started as early as the 32nd week in these type cases because when found early, bed rest helps. Signs of effect on the feto-placental unit would be change in placental grade (new work in the early 1980s and not a standard here applied), failure of growth of the fetus (intrauterine growth retardation, or IUGR—there are norms of what to expect), and diminution on the volume of amniotic fluid. A clinical indication of retardation of growth can be had from fundal measurements (measuring the uterine height above the maternal symphysis pubis) that are less than expected. The proper standard now and in 1983 was serial ultrasound. Intrauterine growth retardation (IUGR) or suspected IUGR or oligohydramnios (too little fluid) were important findings of alteration from the normal. These were not done in this case. It was the standard of care in a case such as this where such feto-placental changes were documented to hospitalize the patient and place her at good nutrition in the left lateral position (to improve placental blood flow) and do daily non- stress test. If the fetus showed no recovery or, if it worsened, delivery was indicated. None of this was done in this case before delivery.

If the fetus was in good shape on all of these studies or, in the alternative, if a fetus who was in danger as shown by the sonogram and/or non-stress test and contraction stress test improved in the hospital, there was no reason to deliver as early as was done here. No one would argue against delivery at or after 37 weeks of even a healthy baby by induction—if the true due date was known and Bishop Score appropriate.

5.   Bishop Score:

This is a measurement of the cervical condition and an evaluation of difficulty to be expected with induction of labor. It incorporates cervical length, closure, texture, station of presenting part and a few other variables. In this case the Bishop Score was not computed but the comments of fetal station and cervical condition indicate that it would have been low and that difficulty in induction should be expected. Proper cervical evaluation and computation of the Bishop Score would have altered the prudent physician to be as sure as possible the induction was indicated.

Induction of labor is not a benign procedure. There are several firm induction criteria aimed at the safety of mother and fetus that were not followed in this case. In the case of induction for fetal indication, as was claimed here, there must be adequate documentation that the fetal indication for induction in fact existed. There was no such documentation here and there was no such fetal indication present. The chart renderings to the contract are not to be believed, especially in light of the contents of the pre-dictated notes. In fact, due to the Bishop Score, the condition of the fetus and the unsure date, there were contraindications to induction at this time in this case.

In this case, the claim is made that there was chronic hypertension with superimposed toxemia (pregnancy induced hypertension), and this indicated induction or delivery. To make the case of pregnancy induced hypertension there must be the fulfillment of several criteria, not fulfilled in this case: There must be an elevation of the blood pressure to greater than 150 systolic or 90 diastolic or an increase of 30 systolic and/ or 15 diastolic. This increase must be present on two occasions six hours apart with the patient at rest. These criteria did not occur even once. There must be significant proteinuria (protein in the urine). There was trace proteinuria on a voided specimen (unreliable). There must be neurologic changes (hyperreflexia), significant headache, significant edema and a few other changes. None of these were present.

In close analysis, there was no immediate maternal or fetal indication for immediate delivery. Until the membranes were ruptured, Dr. Hall had a way out of these problems: just stop doing what was not indicated.

In this case, there was an unsure due date as noted. This alone should have prevented induction unless the situation dictated extreme maternal or fetal jeopardy that was documentable and that was not manageable by more conservative methods. In this case, there was no immediate jeopardy, no attempt at conservative management of the purported problems, no documentation of the purported problems and no indication to deliver.

The failure to assess this patient for toxemia or other accelerated forms of hypertension, the failure to assess her fetus for placental problems and the failure to properly assess the actual due date were all below the standard of care.

In this case, the records indicate that the patient was, in fact, earlier in gestation than Dr. Hall thought, in no immediate danger of fetal demise or maternal stroke, and did not respond to induction as would have been predicted. She had an unnecessary C-section.

The attempted induction, as in this case, subjects the fetus to uterine contractions. It is, in effect, a contraction stress test. The reactivity of the fetus to the attempted induction showed that it was not in danger of loss.

Of course, Mrs. Meyer could have needed a C-section at a later date or more problems could have developed, but at the point in time selected for this delivery, they were not in evidence. On the contrary, the indications are that this pregnancy could have gone farther towards maturity without intervention of this sort.

The premature delivery produced a premature child with the brain structure of a preemie. These children have a weaker support system for blood vessels in the brain areas described as damage in this case, and there is, commonly in preemies, breakdown of the vessels and bleeding with subsequent brain damage. The brain is one of the organs that, once damaged, never re-grows. The damaged structures are lost forever. If the pediatric records of this child show a static encephalopathy with symptoms that would be expected to be due to loss of the areas we know to be involved, you have causation:

1.   Substandard assessment and establishment of due date;

2.   Substandard evaluation of this at-risk fetus in 3rd trimester; or, failure to transfer to a better equipped physician;

3.   Substandard evaluation of this mother in 3rd trimester;

4.   Failure to hospitalize her for evaluation and/or conservative management;

5.   Failure to follow standard of care in evaluating for delivery;

6.   Un-indicated C-section;

7.   Un-indicated early delivery.

Resulting in:

> 1. Negligent decision to deliver this patient;
>
> 2. Unnecessary C-section;
>
> 3. Delivery of preemie who then suffered the problems of prematurity, including brain damage.

After you read this, please call to discuss this case. I will give more details as they become available from the additional records I requested.

You will need a practicing obstetrician and a pediatric neurologist as experts.

I spent 6.5 hours on this case at the agreed upon rate of $150.00 per hour, totaling $975.00 to date.

Dr. Allen's opinion seemed to jumpstart our case. Mr. Stone started getting the whole law firm involved. He had attorney Dunkin gathering and reviewing additional medical records and also investigating the current address of Dr. Hall. Paralegals were given a prepared list of medical articles to obtain at a nearby university library.

The next priority became discussions of the possibilities of producing, writing, shooting, and editing a day/life videotape. The weeks ahead involved several discussions with production companies regarding ideas and cost estimates to write and produce such a video. The day/life video would start out with Brenda waking up Brett for school. It would show the daily difficulties of dressing, grooming, bathing, feeding, lifting, toileting a growing eight-year-old boy. The video crew would follow him the entire day until time for bed that night. Costs, and the obstacles of shooting video on the school bus and at school, would need to be ironed out before proceeding further.

Mr. Stone was also in discussions with his partners at the law firm, strategizing on locating medical experts to strengthen our case. Dr. Allen suggested talking to Dr. Bradley Thompson, a pediatric neurology specialist from New York. He had admitting privileges at two hospitals in New York City. Mr. Stone called Dr. Thompson and asked if he would give an appraisal from the pediatric neurology point of view concerning a child who had cerebral palsy. Dr. Thompson said yes. Focus then concentrated on working out Dr. Thompson's retainer and fee demands before sending him the medical records for his expert opinion.

As the Fourth of July quickly approached that year, Brett was finishing up summer school. Gina was twelve years old. We never thought twice when she asked to watch her brother for the remainder of the summer while we were at work. Some financial requests were also to be considered, but we also knew there was no one more responsible, caring, and loving than Gina. Our house had been on the market for several months at that point with minimal interest. Our listing on the house would run out soon, and we would need to decide our next move.

Attorney Dunkin continued working on costs of potential producers of the day/life video. Discussions were also initiated with another potential medical expert, Dr. Russell Burnett, from Los Angeles. His expertise was in obstetric/gynecological care. We now had experts from the East and West Coast working on our case. Both medical experts would spend the next several weeks reviewing the medical records, and both experts would require further information and test results before they could render an expert opinion.

In early August, Mr. Stone contacted us regarding the day/life video. He told us we should expect a call from Bill Beck. "Bill is a writer and television journalist who will write and direct the video that we want to make about Brett's daily life. It will be necessary for him to meet with you so he can gather information and ideas for the production of the video. I know you will give him your complete cooperation."

At first we were thrilled about the video and all the other activity revolving around our case. It was very exciting. Then reality set in. How were we going to explain a production crew following our son around through his daily routine? Small-town gossip would eat this up. Everyone around town knew about our problems with the school district. A video crew following Brett for an entire day was sure to result in several twisted explanations.

The video shoot was scheduled for early October. The school district had several concerns that needed to be worked out before they would allow a video crew into the school. Confidentiality was the main obstacle, and also the school district wanted a copy of the video. Everything was finally ironed out and the video shoot went off on schedule.

When I left for work at 4:45 a.m. on the day of the video shoot, Brenda was already showered and putting on her make-up. The video crew showed up at 6 a.m. They had spent the night at a small motel about ten miles from our home. Why they spent the night in a cheap motel instead of getting up an extra hour early for the drive is beyond me. The crew worked non-stop, catching every aspect of

Brett's daily activities. By the time I arrived home from work later that night, everyone seemed very comfortable with the whole video shoot. After dinner, everyone took a short break, and then the crew interviewed Brenda and me about Brett. The shoot came to a conclusion with Brenda giving Brett a bath and both of us putting him to bed.

The next several weeks involved editing, script, and script voiceover. We received a copy of the video just after Thanksgiving. The twenty-minute production was very emotional for us to watch. The purpose of the video was for exactly that: the video would be used as a settlement tool in our case or for jury sympathy if it went to trial.

Everything involving our daily life was moving at a crazy pace. Christmas was only weeks away. Just about the time we thought things were slowing down enough to enjoy the holidays, another letter came from Mr. Stone. This letter would make us realize just how serious our lives were about to be changed.

Dear Mr. & Mrs. Meyer:

I wish you to give me written authority for purposes of negotiating in your son Brett's case. There are a number of considerations which you must take into account. First, you must remember that this is Brett's case and that you yourselves will have no interest or right to any settlement proceeds. While one of you will undoubtedly be appointed as his guardian, any and all expenditures of the funds (after deduction of attorney's fees and costs of procuring the settlement) will be subject to approval of the trial court and the probate court once the estate is established.

Secondly, you must bear in mind that unless we can settle, we must take our chances with a jury and we must wait several years to find out if we will be better or worse than the offer we might receive from Dr. Hall's insurer.

Then you should also weigh that while we believe that the raw value of your son's case, without considering the question of whether Dr. Hall is or isn't to blame, could be several millions of dollars (we have seen statistics suggesting figures ranging from less than one million to $7,000,000), on the other hand we are told that Dr. Hall has only $1,000,000 in insurance coverage. (We will demand verification of this during our negotiations.) Unless we can find additional defendants who can be held legally liable we will be stuck with this coverage limitation. At this juncture we do not believe that there is any way to add defendants.

Next, you should consider that there is a method which can increase the money available to Brett beyond the one million dollars. This method is to create a "structured" settlement. In a structured settlement the insurance company would buy annuities or bonds or other private or government securities and place them in a trust for Brett in such a fashion that he would receive set payments over his lifetime. The insurer would consider this if it could save some money on its policy. It is possible to arrange a structure that could bring Brett several million over his lifetime instead of only one million over less costs and attorney's fees. Of course, with good investment strategy Brett can do the same thing, but his interest earnings would be taxable when earned if he did it but non-taxable until paid to him under a structured settlement. The other drawbacks are that under a structured settlement there is usually very little front money, usually just enough to pay attorney's fees and costs with perhaps a little left over, and payments to Brett probably wouldn't begin for 2 to 5 years in order to allow the principle to grow before spending begins. If the money is paid in a lump sum settlement Brett can spend whatever the court approves whenever he wants to.

If you are committed to maximizing Brett's funds a lump sum settlement could probably be handled well enough by you through investment counselors to come very close to making up for the tax deferred status of a structured settlement. Of course, the probate court may have to approve the investment program.

Lastly, be sure to include in your thoughts the fact that all attorney's fees and costs will be deducted from Brett's settlement and he will receive the balance. On a one million dollar settlement or verdict his deductions will range from about $350,000 to as much as $475,000 depending on whether suit is filed and how much must be spent in marshaling the evidence and preparing for trial. For example, we have already spent about $10,000 plus/minus in costs just getting this far. Attorney's fees are 1/3 now and will advance to 40% if suit is filed.

We would like your authority to demand as a settlement $4,000,000 or all of the insurance coverage that Dr. Hall has if it is less than $4,000,000 and $10,000 of his own funds. We add the $10,000 of Dr. Hall's own funds because that forces the insurance company to discuss settlement openly and completely with him and gives him an incentive to urge them to settle within their policy limits. If you wish for us to add that you are willing to consider a structured settlement we will do so. We would also like your authority to accept the one million dollars in settlement if that in fact turns out to be the in-surance policy limits available to Dr. Hall. We also want you to be assured that we will consult with you before any settlement is made.

Brenda and I considered all our options over and over. We con-sulted with both our parents about the decision we faced regarding proceeds that could potentially take care of Brett the rest of his life. We knew none of this was a sure thing, but we were very confident with the representation that was fighting for Brett. After great thought, we decided to go with the lump-sum settlement.

CHAPTER 5

The new year started with little activity. Everything was in a holding pattern while Dr. Hall and his insurance carrier considered our demands for a quick settlement. We showed the day/life video to both our families during the holidays. Everyone who watched the production seemed very surprised at how difficult our daily life actually was, especially for Brenda.

Brenda and I were becoming very confident about how the legal case was progressing. It was so exciting following the daily activity revolving around our case. I even started fantasizing about different ways the money could be used. These thoughts would soon come back to reality after we received a letter from Mr. Stone a few weeks later.

Re: Brett Meyer v. Robert Hall, M.D.

Dear Mr. & Mrs. Meyer:

On Wednesday, January 15, 1992, I spoke with Mr. James Thomas, an adjuster for Dr. Hall's insurer. He informed me that under their policy of insurance, Dr. Hall has the right to consent to any settlement which is made. He further advised that Dr. Hall will not at this time consent to any settlement, and therefore the company is not in a position to extend any offer of settlement to us. I advised him, as I am advising you, that under the circumstances we will proceed to file suit immediately and begin our discovery procedure. As soon as we have prepared the lawsuit for filing, I will send you a copy for your comments.

I am so sorry that I cannot bring you happier news. Dr. Hall's attitude is not unusual. Most doctors have a high degree of self-respect and react very defensively when they are accused of malpractice. In addition to that, there is a federal law which requires that all claims against doctors be listed on a federal registry that is available to hospitals in the event that a doctor applies for affiliation. This is making it more and more difficult to settle malpractice cases, because, as the doctors begin to realize that this registry exists, they adopt the attitude that they would rather fight than settle since a settlement goes down in the registry as an adverse result in the same manner that a judgment against them would, and thereby presents a possible obstacle for further hospital affiliation.

We are now launching upon a process which may take another two years or more to complete. Have courage and have patience. We have good experts on our side, and at this point I am very optimistic about our ultimate success.

Please tell Brett that everybody here sends him our warmest regards and that we wish you all a happy new year.

We were very disappointed that a settlement had not been reached. Thoughts started to go through our minds about a future court battle. It would be very difficult going into a courtroom with the doctor sitting across from us. I started to wonder how uncomfortable he would be, looking at us with our son in a wheelchair.

Our first agenda for the new year was to sell our home and move into town. We relisted our house with a new real estate agent. This was the fourth real estate company we had listed with at that point. Her office was located in a small town about ten miles south of our home. She was having much success selling homes with small acreage like ours. One weekend in early March, we received an unusual call from our new agent. The call was to let us know that she was spending the afternoon praying over our listing. This is not a typical call you get from your real estate agent, but we were willing to try anything to sell our home. A week later, she brought us a contract on our house. The offer was just a few thousand dollars less than what we were asking. We accepted the offer! Everything was contingent on financing, home inspection, and an appraisal.

It was time to start looking for our new home. Unfortunately, the home we had wanted to buy was off the market. We asked the realtor who had the former listing to approach the owner and see if they were still interested in selling. They responded with a firm purchasing price and the stipulation that we allow them to rent the house for ninety days while they finished building a new home. We accepted their price and stipulation.

Brenda was able to find a nice three-bedroom house for us to rent for the next three months. We had a great deal of work ahead of us before thinking about moving, though. The biggest problem was getting rid of all the junk stored in our outside sheds. Both sides of our family needed to find new homes for their campers, boats, trailers, and other small equipment. Everything else left behind either went to an auction house or was burned.

On the last Friday in April, our families and closest friends came to the house early that evening for pizza and beer. It would be the last of thousands of meals shared over several generations in the huge farmhouse. A short time later, a long line of pick-up trucks loaded with all our belongings pulled out the long driveway for the last time, headed to our new temporary home.

By the end of that weekend, we were pretty well settled into our new living situation. Most of our furniture and other personal belongings went to a storage facility. We planned on moving into our new home in late July.

It was a big adjustment for me living in town. I had free time. I was used to four or five hours of grass cutting, and another hour of trimming. This yard took twenty minutes to cut and trim. I liked having the grocery and hardware stores a few minutes away. I was enjoying city life.

A few weeks later, we started noticing an unusual amount of correspondence coming from Mr. Stone's law firm. The next step in our legal case was to send the initial pleadings and discovery documents to Dr. Allen. He was the first expert we consulted in the beginning of this case to review the medical records. The legal papers that are filed in court at the beginning of a lawsuit are called pleadings. Discovery is the pre-trial phase in a lawsuit in which each party, through the law of civil procedure, can obtain evidence from the opposing party by means of discovery devices, including requests for answers to interrogatories, requests for production of documents, requests for admissions, and depositions.

Usually, the first document filed in a lawsuit is the complaint or petition. This provides an outline of the plaintiff's case against the defendant. The petition is a document that identifies the parties involved, sets out the legal basis for the court's jurisdiction over the controversy, states the plaintiff's legal claims, and relates the facts given rise to the claims. The petition will also contain a section called a demand for judgment or prayer for relief. Here, the plaintiff will set forth what he or she wants the court to require the defendant to do, such as pay damages. The purpose of the petition is to provide the defendant with notice of the factual and legal bases of the plaintiff's claims.

Dr. Allen returned his proposed pleadings and discovery, combined with the initial proposed pleadings and discovery, which produced the following proposed petition and discovery documents in this case:

PETITION - MEDICAL MALPRACTICE

Plaintiff Brett James Meyer by and through his Next Friends, Natural Guardians and Parents, Brenda Meyer and Keith Meyer, states for his cause of action against Defendant Robert J. Hall, M.D., the following:

1. Plaintiff Brett James Meyer and Brenda Meyer and Keith Meyer were at all times relevant individuals residing in the County of Marshall, State of Missouri. Presently they reside in Marshalltown, Missouri. Brenda Meyer is the natural mother of Brett James Meyer. Keith Meyer is the natural father of Brett James Meyer.

2. Defendant is and was at all times relevant an individual residing in and can be found in the County of Madison, State of Missouri; is licensed to practice medicine and is a health care provider who practices medicine at 6511 West 62nd Avenue, Oakville, Missouri.

3. Venue for this claim is proper in Madison County, Missouri.

4. At all times relevant Defendant Robert J. Hall, M.D., held himself out to the public and to Brenda and

Keith Meyer as having expertise in that specialty of medicine known as obstetrics, and in that capacity was the physician for hire for Brenda Meyer while she was pregnant with Brett James Meyer, and attended her during labor and delivery of that child.

5. Defendant Robert J. Hall, M.D., in his capacity as obstetrician for Brenda Meyer delivered Brett James Meyer by Cesarean section on December 27, 1983. Brett James Meyer is at the time of this pleading eight (8) years of age.

6. Plaintiff Brett James Meyer by and through the decisions and actions of Defendant Robert J. Hall, M.D., was delivered prematurely and was caused to sustain damage as a result thereof.

7. Defendant Robert J. Hall, M.D., was negligent in causing the premature delivery of Plaintiff and Plaintiff's resulting injuries in that he failed to use that degree of skill and learning ordinarily used under the same or similar circumstances by members of the medical profession with similar training in the following respects:

a. Defendant failed to properly assess and establish the due date for Plaintiff Brett James Meyer's delivery or to make timely and accurate assessments of Plaintiff Brett James Meyer's gestational age;

b. Defendant failed to perform the proper clinical and/or laboratory tests such as the roll-over test, evaluation of deep tendon reflexes, sonography for placental grade and location, tests on urine to detect the presence of significantly elevated amount of protein or tests for function of Brenda Meyer's liver and kidneys to assess the medical condition of the mother, Brenda Meyer, in the third trimester of this pregnancy;

c. Defendant failed to perform third trimester fetal growth monitoring through ultrasound, failed to perform amniocentesis, and failed to do tests for the presence of surfactant in the amniotic fluid in order to evaluate the medical condition of Brett James Meyer in order to make a proper determination regarding the need for preterm delivery and the timing of such delivery;

d. Defendant performed an un-indicated Cesarean section to deliver Plaintiff Brett James Meyer;

e. Defendant failed to allow or perform a timely delivery of Plaintiff Brett James Meyer;

f. Defendant failed to confirm the estimated date of confinement for this pregnancy prior to attempted induction of labor;

g. Defendant failed to establish and/or demonstrate the need for induction of labor by use of contemporary scientific methods or analysis;

h. Defendant failed to establish and/or demonstrate the need for Cesarean section delivery at the time it was done by use of contemporary scientific methods or analysis;

8. That as the direct and proximate result of negligence of defendant, Robert J. Hall, M.D., as aforesaid, Plaintiff Brett James Meyer was caused to sustain the following serious, permanent, and progressively disabling injuries: Periventricular leukomalacia in the brain with attendant loss of brain function, hyaline membrane disease, cerebral palsy, paralysis and weakness of the muscles of the torso, limbs and extremities, causing loss of use and the attendant need for special appliances, training and physical care, hemorrhages into the brain, seizures, developmental delay and failure of development of certain physical abilities, developmental delay neurologically and intellectually with permanent loss of certain of those critical functions; Plaintiff Brett James Meyer has been caused to have great pain and suffering

in parts of the body and mind; that all of said injuries are serious, permanent and progressive in nature; and the nature and use of all of said parts of the body and mind are severely impaired and made painful.

9. As a direct and proximate result of Defendant's acts of negligence, Plaintiff Brett James Meyer has incurred medical expenses due to ongoing treatment in the approximate amount of Fifty Thousand Dollars ($50,000.00) and in the future will be caused to incur further expenses for physical care, education, appliance costs, and medical expenses at an amount presently undetermined.

10. As a direct and proximate result of the negligence of Defendant Hall as aforesaid Plaintiff's reasonable life expectancy has been substantially shortened and diminished, and his quality and enjoyment of life has been greatly impaired and reduced.

11. As a direct and proximate result of the negligence of Defendant Hall as aforesaid Plaintiff's future ability to work, labor, and earn a living has been greatly impaired and reduced.

WHEREFORE, Plaintiff Brett James Meyer by and through his Next Friends, Natural Guardians and Parents, pray for judgment against Defendant Robert J. Hall, M.D., in the amount in excess of $15,000.00 that will fairly and reasonably compensate Plaintiff Brett James Meyer for all damages he has incurred and will incur in the future, for the costs of these proceedings, and for such other and further relief as the Court deems just and equitable.

Once the petition was filed with the court and the discovery documents were served upon Dr. Hall, the mud-slinging started. Dr. Hall had Brinkman, Cole, and Winston as his legal representation. Both law firms battled each other with objections regarding interrogatories served upon each other. Interrogatories are a formal set of written questions propounded by one litigant and required to be answered by the adversary in order to clarify matters of fact and help to determine in advance what facts will be presented at any trial in the case. Each side wanted to know what the other side was holding as far as evidence. This process continued for several months.

We finally moved into our new home in the end of July. Brenda and the kids were just minutes from work and school. Unfortunately, it added an extra ten miles to my drive to work each way. The first day of school was just weeks away for the kids, and our relationship with the school district was worse than ever.

Brett's IEP, or Individual Education Plan, meeting was scheduled in two weeks. We had several issues that needed to be addressed with the school district regarding his IEP. An IEP defines the individualized objectives of a child who has been found with a disability, as defined by federal regulations. The IEP is intended to help children reach educational goals more easily than they otherwise would. In all cases, the IEP must be tailored to the individual student's needs as identified by the evaluation process, and it must especially help teachers and related service providers understand the student's disability and how the disability affects the learning process. The IEP describes how the student learns, how the student demonstrates, and what teachers and service providers will do to help the student learn more effectively.

Developing an IEP requires assessing students in all areas related to the known disabilities, simultaneously considering ability to access the general curriculum and how the disability affects the student's learning, forming goals and objectives that correspond to the needs of the student, and choosing a placement in the least restrictive environment possible for the student.

I was beginning to think these meetings were a waste of time. The school district was good at making promises about services for Brett. Following through with these services never happened, though. The IEP was supposed to be a contract between us and the district regarding these services. We even started recording the meetings to protect Brett's rights. The school district came prepared with their own recorder.

Our main concerns were getting Brett integrated into classes part of the day with normal children his age. We considered this the "least restrictive environment." The district policy in the past was to place the disabled and problem kids at the one end of the building, away from the other children.

Another big problem concerned some of the related services. We were very satisfied with speech therapy. Brett's communication skills were improving every day. The school district was failing to follow through with the proper physical and occupational therapy services. These were serious violations to his IEP. As parents, this was the only protection we had to fall back on.

In one IEP meeting, we brought up that none of the schools in the district had handicap parking. The school district's answer to this problem was "Call us when you're coming to an activity, and we will have someone let you in the back door."

CHAPTER 6

1993 started off with a very big surprise. Brenda came home one evening after work with great news. She told Brett that she received a phone call that day from the Make-A-Wish Foundation. Brenda said, "Brett, the foundation is granting you a wish." Brett just sat there with a smile on his face. Brenda and I quickly realized that he didn't understand how special this was. We were all so excited for Brett! I was kind of puzzled about the whole situation. I thought only terminally ill children were granted wishes like this. Brenda said someone was going to come to our house in a few weeks to talk to Brett about his wish.

The lady from the foundation came to our home to grant his wish a few weeks later. She asked Brett, "What is your wish?"

Brett thought about it and said, "I want to go on a trip." She asked where to, and he replied, "I don't care, just a trip where I can go swimming."

She said, "How would you feel about taking your mom, dad, and sister to see Mickey Mouse in Florida?"

"I would like that! I like that a lot!"

The Make-A-Wish Foundation was going to fly the four of us to Orlando, Florida. A rental vehicle would be provided by Budget for us to get around the area. We would stay in a cottage on a property called Give Kids the World Village. An accessible pool would be just outside the cottage door for Brett to swim. We would all have unlimited access to Disney World, Universal Studios, and Sea World. This was just a small part of everything Brett and the rest of us would have in store. It was going to be a dream trip for all of us. Brett's wish trip was going to be in late May. We couldn't wait!

With the good news also came some bad. My older brother, Gary, had been going to a dermatologist for some unusual skin rashes. After treating him for a short length of time, the dermatologist recommended he be seen by specialists at the University School of Medicine. They diagnosed his condition as a very rare malignancy of the skin. My brother really didn't talk much at first about the diagnosis.

Gary and I worked for the same construction company. He actually helped me get my present job. I had been laid off for a short time when my brother called and said his boss needed a laborer for some demolition work. He told me it was only going to amount to three days of work. The three days turned into eight years and counting now. We usually worked on the same job sites even though he was a carpenter and I was a laborer.

Even though we were working and commuting together to the same job, I was having a hard time getting any information about his skin problems. This was not unusual. Gary never talked much about his problems or personal life. He pretty well lost everything getting divorced several years earlier, including custody to his daughter, Amanda. He had rights to see her every other weekend, but it was still tough to swallow. Because of his financial and medical issues, he was forced into asking our parents for help. Of course they helped him out. He moved back into their home until he could get back on his feet.

One Friday night as we were driving home from work, we stopped off and had a few beers. After my brother finished his third beer, he began to loosen up and talk about his problems. He let some things slip about his medical condition. I was shocked to find out his doctor had told him to get his affairs in order. "What do you mean, get your affairs in order?" I said. "You told me this was treatable." He told me to relax, that everything was okay and the treatments were working. My only choice was to believe him, but I was going to start watching him a lot closer.

Our legal case was still moving along—very slow but sure. All the interrogatory objections had been ruled on by the court, and both sides were satisfied with the information they required. Depositions became the focus of both sides. Our depositions were scheduled for late September.

The day finally arrived for Brett's dream trip. We flew out of St. Louis on a Friday. The airport was very busy because it was the start of the Memorial Day weekend. This was going to be Gina and Brett's first experience on a plane. I wondered how it was going to work with the wheelchair. They allowed us to have early boarding. When we arrived at the end of the jetway, the ground crew took the wheelchair and put it with the baggage underneath the plane. I carried Brett to our seats in row twenty-one. It was very difficult carrying him down such a narrow aisle.

We left St. Louis on schedule. Everything went great until about an hour into the flight. Brett decided he needed to go to the restroom. I started to ask him if he could wait until we got to Orlando, when Brenda gave me the evil eye. I picked him up and carried him towards the restroom, bouncing off people's shoulders and seat backs all the way up the aisle. Of course, when we arrived at the door, it said occupied. I looked back towards our seat and noticed about a hundred people wondering why I was standing at the front of the plane holding my nine-year-old son. The door finally opened. As the person exited the restroom, we had to do a little dance to allow each other to pass. I looked back towards Brenda and Gina again and noticed a hundred and fifty people watching us.

I then looked into the restroom. How were both of us going to fit in this small area? I lowered Brett to his feet, turning him around to face away from me, and picked him up to go in. We both fit, but there wasn't enough room to close the door. Stepping back to take a look on how this was going to work, I looked again towards the back of the plane. We now had two hundred people watching!

"Brett, you're going to have to help," I said. I stepped back through the door and lifted him up, telling him to stand on top of the toilet for a second while I tried to close the door.

Giggling, he said, "Okay!" I finally got the door closed!

I pulled down his shorts and underpants and positioned him so he could pee. Suddenly, someone knocked on the door. I called out, "Just a minute!" Brett started giggling again. I wondered how this person couldn't have seen us go through the juggling act to even be in this tight compartment. I told Brett to hurry up. I stood there supporting Brett, wishing he would get this over with. Another loud knock sounded from the other side of the door. I wanted to open the door so bad just to see who this idiot was, but I knew it wouldn't work at that point. This time I yelled, "Wait a minute!" Brett was now laughing.

I asked, "Do you need to go or not?"

Brett looked up at me and said, "I'll wait."

When I opened the door, the knocker was gone.

When our flight landed in Orlando, it was just before noon. After getting our luggage, we made our way to Budget for our vehicle. Everything was moving along very smoothly. They walked us out to a minivan. I put the luggage behind the two rear captain chairs and secured Brett in his seat. I opened up the rear hatch to load the wheelchair. It wouldn't fit! I took the wheel's off the frame, and it still didn't fit. I worked and worked and could not make it work.

I walked back to the desk. The gentleman asked me if something was wrong with the vehicle. I told him our problem with the wheelchair. He looked at me and said "What vehicle will work? Do you think a Ford Explorer will work?"

I said, "I guess that would work, but this is through the Make-A-Wish Foundation. I don't know if I'm allowed to make any changes to our itinerary."

"Sir, Budget will provide any vehicle you desire while you're in Orlando for your son," the gentleman said.

"Thank you!" I said. "Thank you so much!"

After a short drive, we arrived at Give Kids the World Village. It truly was the wonderful, magical, and magnificent place we had all dreamed about. Here is the official, authorized—and bunnyized—tale of Give Kids the World Village as told by Clayton the Rabbit, mayor of the village.

> Once upon a time, a man named Henri Landwirth ran a hotel near Walt Disney World. Each year, thousands of children came to Florida to bask in the warm sunshine and enjoy all the things to do. And many of them stayed at Henri's hotel.

> One day, Henri learned of a special little girl who also wanted to come to Florida to play. But the girl was very sick. For her family to come to Florida was an incredible challenge. Henri wanted to help. He said the little girl could come stay at his hotel.

Then Henri learned that more children wanted to come. So Henri went to all his friends and asked them to help him bring these special children to Florida. Soon, families from all around the world were arriving in Orlando and had the opportunity meet Mickey Mouse and visit Walt Disney World. Henri knew all these children needed a special place to stay. Henri set out on a search to find the land to build his village. And when he went looking, he found me, Clayton the Rabbit. I brought him to the land where he would build the 35-acre resort called Give Kids the World Village.

Soon, villas for the children and families sprung up everywhere. And the children started coming from all over. And I loved them. I became so close with many of the children that they elected me mayor for life. Can you believe that? They elected a rabbit as the head of the village. And as mayor, I've witnessed so much magic at the village. Some may even call them miracles.

In the center of the village, we cut away some overgrown vines only to find a magic castle hidden beneath, filled with magic mirrors, enchanted wishing wells, and a talking grandfather clock. On another night, a little boy hid his last gingerbread cookie beneath a stone near the castle for the next day. When the sun broke the next morning, an entire gingerbread house had risen on the spot, filled with bountiful treats to delight children of all ages.

Give Kids the World built this village just for you. Your official duty as a citizen of the village during your stay is to have fun. And may all your dreams come true!

Brett absolutely loved the village. I have to admit it was very impressive. Our cottage, or villa, was very spacious. It had three bedrooms and two full bathrooms. The fridge was filled with different beverages and small snack dinners. A large pool was just outside our patio door for Brett. There was a merry-go-round that even accommodated his wheelchair. The gingerbread house and talking grandfather clock fascinated Brett. A small train car was located on the property that could be visited at any time during the day for ice cream. It was paradise! The whole trip was an experience of a lifetime. At least, most of it was. Brett absolutely loved the resort, especially the big swimming pool. The water gave him the freedom to act like anyone else. He was free to kick his legs and move everywhere, instead of being belted into a wheelchair all day.

Some of the other activities didn't go as well. Our first full day involved going to Disney World. Since it was the holiday weekend, it was very crowded. That really wasn't the problem, though. Brett had a badge on his shirt that allowed us to proceed to the front of any line. When we got on a ride and it started, Brett would freak out. I think this was the first time I realized Brett had visual problems. He was using all his other senses, especially his hearing, to get him through each ride. It was a nightmare. We ended up staying at Disney World a total of three hours.

Brenda and I were both shocked. Brett was visibly shaken by the rides at the amusement park. We looked at each other and knew we needed to leave. We felt so sorry for Gina. As much as she wanted to stay, I believe she also realized we needed to leave.

When we arrived at our vehicle, we just sat there for a few minutes. I wondered what the heck happened. Brett was not throwing a temper tantrum over not getting his way. I could tell he was terrified by the rides we had put him on. Brett wanted to go back to the village and swim. Brenda suggested that we go to Universal Studios. She told Brett that the Ninja Turtles were there. He loved that idea.

Everything was going better at Universal. Brett loved the show with the Ninja Turtles. We went to a few other shows before we came to the *Jaws* ride. It didn't look that bad. It kind of resembled a huge pontoon boat. Brett loved riding on boats. Of course, we immediately went to the front of the line as the next boat approached. We were seated in the middle of about forty people.

I should've known things were going to go wrong when our guide boarded the boat holding a rifle. I was impressed with how Brett was handling the ride after the great white shark appeared a few times. Suddenly, the shark reappeared, and our guide started yelling and firing shots at the great white. The boat hit a telephone pole, and a high voltage wire dropped down to the water. The shark surfaced and bit down on the high voltage wire. After a loud explosion, a mass of steam hit the boat. When I looked down at Brett, he was terrified. His glasses were filled with steam. I could hear him yelling, "I'm done! I've had enough! Get me out of here!"

When the four of us got off the ride, I told Brenda we needed to leave. Brenda just looked at me. I said, "This is Brett's dream trip, not ours." We took Brett back to the cottage, got him an ice cream, and put him in the pool. Life was back to normal.

The next day we planned to go to the ocean and spend the day on the beach. After arriving, we quickly found that Brett's wheelchair wouldn't navigate the terrain. It just sank into the soft sand. I ended up carrying Brett about fifty yards down to the ocean. I sat him so the waves would rush up to him. He quickly rolled over and tried to crawl further out into the water. Within a minute, he was completely covered with sand. I tried to carry him out further into the surf to rinse him off, but he was too heavy and slippery to handle.

By the time I got him back to his wheelchair, I was exhausted. We were both covered with sand. It was a nightmare! This trip was showing us what obstacles were ahead of us in the future.

Sitting at the airport waiting to board our flight home, I reflected on our days in Florida. I couldn't believe it was already time to go home. It was very humbling meeting and talking with other parents from all around the country who were handling much more serious problems with their children than we were with our own. Brett really enjoyed his trip. Sure, we hit a few obstacles. We just adapted and made it work.

I took Brett into the airport restroom just before we boarded our flight home. Hopefully he wouldn't need to use the restroom on our return flight.

The flight home went well until we were just outside St. Louis. The pilot announced we would be landing in about fifteen minutes. When I looked out the window, it seemed like we were still at a pretty high altitude to be landing in ten to fifteen minutes. The plane started descending at an unusually rapid pace. My ears were popping. Glancing over at Brett, I was shocked to see blood shooting out his nose in spurts. I don't know what I said, but within seconds Brenda, Gina, and a flight attendant were hovering over us. I jammed a pillow up against Brett's face to stop the blood flow. I'm surprised he could even breathe. The nosebleed stopped as quickly as it started. A few minutes later, the plane landed and the dream trip was over.

It was hard getting back into a normal routine after such an awesome trip. The rest of the summer would be spent dealing with the great floods of 1993. Even though no river or streams were close to our home, we still felt the effects of the torrential rains that summer. Every time it rained, it seemed to drop three, four, or five inches at a time. One night it rained so hard that the sump pump couldn't keep up and flooded our basement with several inches of water. We had just completed finishing half the basement. Our new carpet and furniture were completely soaked.

Driving back and forth to work every day, my brother and I were amazed about how high the Missouri River was getting. It had never been this high in our lifetime. I remember driving home the Friday afternoon just hours before the Monarch Levee gave way and flooded the entire Chesterfield bottoms. The Missouri River looked like a huge lake as we drove down the hill into the river bottoms and approached the bridge. Later that evening, the whole area flooded. This left only one bridge to get into the St. Louis area. It was going to be a traffic nightmare for weeks.

My dad figured he would be getting a call from his superiors any day because of all the damage the floods were creating along both the Missouri and Mississippi Rivers. My dad had retired about five years earlier. He took and passed the government test to work for the Federal Emergency Management Agency, or FEMA. He had been called out on several natural disasters over those five years. His job involved accessing damage to public facilities after major hurricanes, tornados, ice storms, etc. We all loved listening to the stories and experiences from his many travels.

When the call came, he wasn't surprised. He was instructed to pick up a government vehicle and given several counties along the Mississippi River north of St. Louis. He worked several weeks accessing damage from the floods. He was looking forward to finishing up work on this disaster and enjoying the new pontoon boat him and my mother had recently purchased. The boat was set up for fishing. My parents loved spending their free time doing just that. The only problem with their new purchase was that it would not fit into the pole barn next to the house. My dad planned on fixing that problem during the approaching Labor Day weekend.

When the holiday weekend finally arrived, Brenda and I had plans of our own. We were going to spend Saturday getting caught up around the house. Sunday, we were going to spend the day in our ski boat on the lake with another couple. Gina was going to stay with Brett to give us an adult day out. It would probably be our last chance to use the boat before cold weather. Our depositions were also scheduled for the end of September. Mr. Stone had scheduled several appointments with us to start reviewing information to help us prepare.

I will never forget that Sunday morning. I had gotten up early to pick up our boat from storage and had started going through my normal routine and maintenance. I remember hearing the phone ringing from the garage and walking inside to answer it. It was my dad. I told him about our plans for the day, and he told me to have a good time but to be careful. In the back of my mind I thought he wanted me to come help him and my brother work on his shed that day. They had worked the day earlier, extending the shed out with a higher roof so the new boat would fit.

Brenda and I were just getting ready to pull out of the driveway when Gina came running out to stop us. "Dad! Dad! Wait!" she yelled. "Gary is on the phone, and something is wrong!"

I ran into the house and picked up the phone. "What's wrong, Gary?" I asked.

"Get down here!" he yelled. "Get down here now! Dad fell off the shed roof."

"Is he alright?"

"I called for an ambulance!" my brother replied. "It's not good. Just get down here!"

When I ran out the garage door, Brenda asked, "What's wrong?"

"Dad fell off the shed roof! It's not good!" I yelled. "Gina, take care of your brother!" I quickly disconnected the boat, and we headed to my parents' house.

Even though it was only a fifteen-minute drive, it was still the longest drive of my life. Many thoughts rushed through my head about what injuries my dad could have sustained. Could it be a broken leg or legs, a broken arm? When we pulled up to their home, my thoughts quickly turned into fear. I can still remember Brenda saying "Oh crap!"

There were two ambulances backed into the field between the house and the barn. Brenda and I ran up and watched them work on my dad. My brother was a mess. Gary said, "I called Mom at church. She's on her way home!" The paramedics told us that they had called for a helicopter to transport our dad to the nearest trauma center. We could see the helicopter approaching as my mother pulled into the driveway.

My dad was still conscience as my mom rushed to his side with tears in her eyes. He wasn't able to talk to her, but I know he knew she was at his side. The helicopter landed just yards from us. The medical team rushed in as the pilot stayed back, standing next to his flying machine. The chopper blades were still turning at a rapid rate, ready to rush my dad to the hospital. I could see my parents' neighbors standing at a distance, trying to figure out what happened.

At this point, six people were working on my dad, assessing his injuries. They were cutting his clothes away and marking different spots on his body as potential injuries. He had a huge lump on his forehead. Apparently he hit his head on something during the fall or when he hit the ground. I could tell his condition was rapidly deteriorating. I remember one paramedic looking up at us and shaking his head.

The medical team rushed my dad into the helicopter. As it lifted off, we loaded into my mom's car and headed for the hospital. It was a forty-five-minute drive. The helicopter probably made it in fifteen. When we arrived at the hospital, we parked and quickly made our way into the emergency room. The nurse at the desk told us to follow her to a small room next to the waiting room. Something didn't seem right to me. Why were we in this small room instead of the waiting room?

The emergency room doctor walked into the small room where

we were waiting. He had a very serious look on his face. He spoke to my mom. "The injuries from the fall your husband sustained were very severe, especially to his head. The medical team worked very hard but... I'm very sorry to tell you he did not pull through. I'm so sorry for your loss."

The doctor stayed with us as the emotions poured out. After a short time passed, he took us into the treatment room where they had worked so hard to save my dad. We all stood looking down at his battered body. Words alone cannot describe the love and respect I had for my dad, and now he was gone.

The sudden death of my father really messed me up. Instead of showing a lot of emotion, I was the complete opposite. My dad had talked to me several times during my lifetime regarding his eventual demise. His wishes were very clear: Take care of your mother, and watch out for your older brother.

We made it through the funeral with the help of family and friends. I knew the weeks ahead were going to be very tough on all of us, especially my mom. It made me feel better knowing my brother would be living under the same roof to keep an eye on her.

The weeks ahead were exceptionally hard on me. I was going to miss our daily conversations about world events, the economy, politics, and just life in general. I could see very dark clouds on the horizon that would be affecting us in the near future, and for the first time in my life I was going face the storm without him.

Several weeks later, I found an old Christmas card in a drawer I was going through. It happened to be from the Christmas before my dad died. The card was from my mom and dad. In the card was a short note from my dad that I will always treasure.

> Needless to say we are very proud of you guys! We love and admire you all as much as a Mom & Dad and Gram & Gramp can possibly express.

> Best wishes for a Healthy, Happy and Prosperous New Year!

> Count Your Blessings!

CHAPTER 7

The dark clouds I could see on the horizon were quickly approaching. Several things were bothering me about upcoming events and circumstances. Number one on my list was concerning my brother. I knew he wasn't telling us everything regarding his declining health. Because I worked on the same job with him, I could see his condition declining every day. When I would question him about the treatments he was going through, he always told me everything was going great.

One day his whole body would look like it was on fire or like it had a very bad sunburn. The next day he would be itching from head to toe like he had poison ivy. That was followed by days of shedding skin like a snake. It was nasty. I could tell the poor guy was in misery.

The next thing bothering me was the approaching lawsuit. We had started the battle over six years ago. Both sides were getting ready to declare war against each other. I was beginning to stress about the costs, which were skyrocketing every day. Our account balance was approaching twenty thousand dollars, and this amount would double in the months ahead due to the costs of travel involved in getting depositions from experts all over the country. We were also responsible for costs associated with the experts' time giving their depositions. These costs would also be very expensive.

The day arrived for our depositions. Brenda and I were the first scheduled to be questioned. Hopefully we were prepared for the questions drilled by the opposing attorney. Our answers would either help our situation, or they could be used against us if our case went before a jury at trail. I was very confident with our attorney and the experts he had found. Let the war begin.

Just before our scheduled depositions, we received the following letter from Mr. Stone:

Dear Keith & Brenda:

We have previously talked about Dr. Hall's insurance coverage being only $1,000,000.00, and you know my view that the reasonable verdict in Brett's case may be $4,000,000.00 or even more. We have also talked about the risks of winning or losing or getting less than $1,000,000.00 from the jury. No scenario can be excluded from our thinking.

There are two basic strategies that we can adopt to deal with this problem of low insurance coverage. Both strategies have their pitfalls and risks, so think carefully about them. Here they are.

1. We can pursue the doctor personally for payment out of his personal assets, or

2. We can offer to settle for the $1,000,000.00 policy limits, and if the insurance company refuses, we then will work to get a verdict larger than the policy limits. If that happens, we will maneuver to take over the doctor's right to sue his insurance company for having refused in bad faith to settle for their policy limits.

Now, let's talk about how these strategies would work and what some of their risks and benefits are. The first strategy is not difficult, but it does not offer great chance of success. Under that strategy, we simply proceed with our lawsuit and let the chips fall where they will. If we succeed in getting a judgment in excess of the insurance coverage, we would then attempt to seize whatever assets the doctor may have. This course would not offer any realistic chance of settlement over the policy limits because the doctor will probably not wish to voluntarily pay out of his own pocket either before or after the verdict. Furthermore, the doctor can use many strategies to make himself "judgment proof." For example, he can hide assets in other people's names. The doctor may not have enough personal wealth to make a large difference in the outcome in any event.

The second strategy, while risky, is more promising than the first, in my opinion. If an insurance company has an opportunity to settle for policy limits and it unreasonably refuses to do so, the insured (Dr. Hall), can sue the company if he gets stuck with a verdict over the policy limits. The doctor would, if successful, use that money to pay off the judgment. In order to set the stage for this to happen, we would be required to make an offer to settle for the policy limit ($1,000,000.00) and keep the offer open for a reasonable period of time (say 45 to 60 days). If it refuses to pay at the end of the time period, we withdraw the offer and go on to trial in due course. Then the stage is set. If we are successful in getting a verdict for more than the policy limits, we then approach the doctor, through his personal attorney if he has one, and ask for the right to sue the insurance company in his shoes to collect the amount over the policy limits. In exchange, we would promise the doctor that we would do nothing to collect from him until we finish the claim against the insurance company. That suit would probably be settled by the insurance company because it would not want to face another jury after it had passed up a reasonable chance to settle.

The first risk in this strategy is that the insurance company might offer to pay the $1,000,000.00 when we demand it. We would then have to take it and that is all we would get. Of course, that is not too terrible a risk because it isn't chicken feed, and even though we have a reasonable chance to get a much bigger verdict, we might not have such a good chance of collecting it from the doctor.

The second risk is that the insurance company might offer the money after the deadline but before the trial. We would not be obliged to take the offer, but if it offers the policy limits, no one could sue for bad faith.

We may get a verdict less than or equal to $1,000,000.00 if we go to trial. That, of course, would eliminate any chance to get a larger amount. Once the insurance company offers the policy limits, it is unlikely that it will withdraw the offer, and we could probably choose to accept it before trial if that is your wish.

The insurance company may possibly offer less than the policy limit. If that came to pass, I would recommend that you go to trial. You, of course, would have the right to settle despite my recommendation.

Lastly, the insurance company may not make an offer. Then there is no choice to make. We go to trial.

What I need to know is whether you are willing for me to attempt strategy number two. That means you would be willing to accept $1,000,000.00 as a total settlement if they should meet our settlement demand. Please answer in writing.

We agreed to go along with Mr. Stone's recommendation and go with strategy number two.

Our depositions were set for the morning of September twenty-second. Both of us felt very nervous as we entered our attorney's office. The receptionist took us to a conference room where Dunkin, the associate attorney who had been helping with our case, and the defendant's insurance attorney, Mr. Brinkman, were waiting. Brenda was sworn in first and waited for Mr. Brinkman to start questioning her.

"Mrs. Meyer, I'm going to ask you some questions about Dr. Hall and the treatment that you received, about yourself, about Brett. If you don't understand any question I ask, will you stop me and ask me to clarify it?"

Brenda answered, "Yes, I will."

Mr. Brinkman continued. "Because I'll assume if you've answered it that you believe you understood the question, okay?"

Brenda again answered yes.

The questioning started. At first, the questions seemed rather simple. He asked for information about the three of us, where we lived, where we worked, and about our jobs, especially Brenda's. Soon the questions switched to Brett's condition, his functioning levels, all the doctors that were treating him and what they were treating him for. Mr. Brinkman wanted exact dates of surgeries and evaluations. Brenda was having a hard time remembering. She handled it very well by just answering "I don't remember."

Suddenly the questions turned to Brenda. Mr. Brinkman began drilling her about her medical history, her family's medical history, and my family's medical history. "Mrs. Meyer, I want to ask you some questions about your pregnancy. Dr. Russell of course was the physician taking care of your needs primarily when you learned you were pregnant as I recall."

"No," Brenda answered. "When I learned I was pregnant, I first went to Dr. Mason. Dr. Russell did not care for my pregnancy."

"He related in his records a positive test, and there were two pregnancy tests done in that summer. One turned positive," Brinkman said. "Was he relating something that someone did, or did he perform it?"

"Dr. Russell did perform that," Brenda answered.

"Was that the first confirmation that you were pregnant, and was the positive pregnancy test performed by Dr. Russell?" Mr. Brinkman asked.

"Yes, it was," Brenda replied.

As I sat and listened to the questions, I couldn't figure out why Brinkman was so fixated on who made the determination that she was pregnant. She did find out she was pregnant after she took the test while working for Dr. Russell. That was one of the perks of her job. Dr. Russell was also our family doctor.

I thought Brenda was doing a great job. I could tell she was starting to feel good about how the depositions were proceeding, but suddenly everything changed.

Mr. Brinkman asked Brenda about the blood pressure medication she was taking during her pregnancy. The drug was called Corgard. Brenda had started taking the prescription just after giving birth to Gina. Dr. Hall tried to switch Brenda to another medication, but she was unable to tolerate the change.

I worried that Brinkman knew something about this drug that our team overlooked. Mr. Brinkman asked, "Has anyone up to this date, any of the physicians you've seen, and I'm not asking you to tell me what the lawyer has told you, but have any of the physicians you've seen, any of the physicians that Brett has seen, indicated or complained that Corgard may have caused injury to Brett?"

"No, they have not," Brenda responded.

"Have any physicians named any medications as being responsible for Brett's condition?" Brinkman asked.

Ms. Dunkin quickly jumped in. "Let me just get an objection in here. She cannot testify as to what is in any medical record. I suppose what you are really asking is have they said that to her. But your question is vague in that respect. Subject to that objection, if you are able to answer, go ahead and do so, Mrs. Meyer."

Brenda again said, "No, they have not."

"What information has any physician provided to you, yours or Brett's or anybody that you yourself asked?" Brinkman asked. "What have you been told about the cause of Brett's disability and condition?"

"Are you asking me what they are telling me is the cause...of the cerebral palsy?" Brenda asked, seeming puzzled by the question. "The doctors have said something to the effect of the prematurity and the brain hemorrhage."

Mr. Brinkman continued to ask several more questions regarding any physician making any statements to her giving any reason for Brett's cerebral palsy. He also asked if any physicians treating Brenda or Brett, or any others she inquired about, expressed any opinions as to the treatment rendered by Dr. Hall.

Brenda answered, "No, they have not."

"Does that include Dr. Russell?" Brinkman asked.

"Yes," she answered.

"Does Dr. Russell know you're suing Dr. Hall?" Brinkman asked.

Brenda said, "Yes, he does."

His questions about what Dr. Russell knew continued. "Has he expressed to you any opinions about as to whether you should or shouldn't be suing Dr. Hall? Have you asked Dr. Russell or any other doctors about the treatment rendered by Dr. Hall?"

"No, I have not." Brenda answered.

"Has Dr. Hall made any statements or comments to you that you took to mean that his treatment of you was somewhat deficient or that some error or mistake was made?" Brinkman asked.

"Only when I think about it now," Brenda responded. "He kept coming in my room after the baby was born saying 'I'm so sorry, Brenda. I'm so sorry.'"

Mr. Brinkman seemed to become defensive at her answer. "You had had a child by that time that was obviously having problems," he stated. "Except for saying he was sorry, did you ask him what he meant by that, or did he say what he meant? Did you assume that by him saying he was sorry that this somehow meant he did something wrong?"

"No, I did not assume that," Brenda quickly said. She also seemed to be getting agitated.

"But, in retrospect, you have been thinking about that apparently?" Brinkman quickly fired back.

Brenda looked him straight in the eye and said, "I've been thinking about it."

Brinkman quickly changed the mood and questioning. He went back through Dr. Hall's records to the point when Brenda started seeing him as a patient. I think he was testing to see how good her memory was because every question would end with "does that sound about right?" Brenda replied to each question saying "yes" or "I don't recall."

This part was killing me. I sat there listening to the questions and immediately knew the answer. I can still think back to that period of time and tell you what happened each day. It was still very clear in my mind. Brenda was the complete opposite. It wasn't her fault, though. Most people can't remember day-by-day circumstances that happened ten years earlier.

Brinkman wanted to know if Brenda kept or prepared any kind of a log or record of visits to Dr. Hall's office or of conversations with him with notes that were made at or about the time the things were happening. Brenda responded that she had no such log or record.

"Do you remember your first visit to Dr. Hall's office?" Mr. Brinkman asked.

"Yes, I do," Brenda replied.

"Did Dr. Hall take any kind of tests or do anything to confirm that you were pregnant?" Brinkman continued.

"I cannot remember," Brenda answered.

"Did he confirm that you were?" he asked.

"Yes, he did," Brenda replied.

"And when did you tell him your last menstrual period was? Do you remember that?" Brinkman asked.

Brenda said, "I believe I told him it was around April eleventh, but I'm not sure about that."

Brinkman sped up the pace again with his questions. "And is that what you told him also, that you weren't real sure?"

"Yes," Brenda responded.

"Let me ask you if there is any documentation of any kind anywhere made at or about the time that you had that menstrual period as to the date of it?" he asked. "And let me clarify what I'm trying to find out. Is there any notation that was made by you at the time, or a trip to the drug store, or maybe a day off work, is there any way that we can look for some documentation that would confirm when you had that last menstrual period?"

Brenda said, "I don't recall having any documentation."

"Since that last visit to his office, have you since tried to determine in some way to confirm that that indeed was the date of your last menstrual period, April eleventh?" Brinkman continued.

"I don't remember," Brenda replied.

Mr. Brinkman asked Brenda several questions about her menstrual periods around the time she became pregnant. He wanted to know if her periods were usually very regular as far as time-wise, were they always so many days apart and the like. Brenda told him she was regular when she was on birth control pills and after that she could not remember.

He asked her if she intentionally stopped taking the birth control pills so she could become pregnant. Brenda told him she did stop taking the pill but did not know a specific date. Brenda said it had been less than a year.

Mr. Brinkman thumbed through his papers. "Let me ask about when you were there that first visit. He shows at the top of the flow sheet that he had the last menstrual period of April eleventh, which is what you have told me already."

Brenda said, "Yes."

"And that the EDC, your estimated date of confinement or delivery being January eighteenth of 1984," he said. "Did he tell you that at that time, on your first or second visit, that he thought your delivery date would be around January eighteenth?"

Brenda looked confused by the question. "I believe so," she said.

Brinkman leaned forward and asked, "Were there ever any other conversations with him about the delivery date other than being January eighteenth of '84? Were there any uncertainties discussed? What do you remember about that?"

Brenda still looked confused. "Are you talking about the beginning of my pregnancy or later on?"

"At any time," Brinkman said.

"He just kept telling us if we can make it until the end of December…" Brenda tried to explain. "I mean, he kept really focusing on us making it until the end of December. We primarily knew our baby would be born at the end of December. He just kept stressing to make it to the end of December."

Brinkman quickly changed the subject. He continued to go through specific dates with Brenda regarding visits to Dr. Hall's office. He mentioned a July thirtieth visit and also one on September third. He asked Brenda if she remembered the September third visit in particular, and Brenda said she didn't. Brinkman asked her if she remembered having an ultrasound on that date. Again, she answered no.

"As you sit here, do you remember any ultrasound being given to you?" he asked.

"Yes, I do," Brenda said.

"He wrote on that entry that there was no quickening. I think that means maybe the baby moving," he shared before continuing. "Do you recall when it was you first felt the baby move?"

"No, I don't," Brenda answered.

"The flow sheet indicates September twenty-sixth. Does that sound right to you?"

"I do not remember," Brenda replied.

Mr. Brinkman leaned back in his chair and said, "I hope you understand that my suggesting these dates to you is not to get you to say something. I'm hoping maybe it might refresh your recollection. Okay?"

Brenda smiled and said, "Yes, I understand."

The next question was "Do you recall discussing with him when you first felt the baby move on the visit, whenever that occurred?"

"I don't remember," Brenda responded.

"Do you remember him at any time telling you that the date you first reported the baby moving had any effect of any kind on the age of the fetus or the due date?" he asked.

"No, I do not," Brenda answered.

"Up through the September third visit, as far as you were concerned, were you worrying about any problems at all?" Brinkman continued.

"None whatsoever," Brenda responded.

"You had had one pregnancy at this point?" he asked. "Was anything different about this one up to that point?"

Brenda tried to hold back a yawn and then answered, "No, there was not."

Suddenly I found myself trying to hold back a yawn before his next question. "Had you been taking medication during your first pregnancy?"

"I don't remember," Brenda replied.

"Through the September third visit, do you remember feeling any apprehension or worry about any condition of either yours or of the fetus?" he asked.

"I was not worried," Brenda responded.

Brinkman continued on, asking questions about the next office visit on October first. He said the record showed Brenda had a second ultrasound at the time. Brenda vaguely remembered what happened during that visit. Brinkman's next question woke me up and made my wheels begin to turn. He asked Brenda if she recalled any conversations about the ultrasound, what it showed in regard to age of the baby, or the sex, or the due date. Brenda of course responded that she did not remember.

I sat there wondering why he was asking all these questions about the ultrasounds. Then I started thinking about some of the questions he had asked Brenda earlier in her deposition. He had asked her if she had kept a log or record of her visits to Dr. Hall, and she had said that she had not.

I had a record of her visits. I had a log of her visits to Dr. Hall's office. I paid the bills for those visits. I even had a record of all the ultrasounds Dr. Hall performed. After each ultrasound, Brenda brought home a picture of our unborn child. Each one had the gestational age of the baby printed on the face of the picture. Originally, I had the pictures filed until we approached Mr. Stone and started the investigation regarding the cause of Brett's disability. I had given those pictures to Mr. Stone.

"The next office note is from November thirtieth," Brinkman continued. "You were complaining of a three-day history of a clear-ish-white discharge present most of the time and increased urinary frequency, but no urgency. Do you remember a visit in which you had those complaints?"

"Vaguely," Brenda answered.

Brinkman said, "On that visit, he notes 'patient also states she has felt no fetal movement at all today,' which would be November thirtieth, 'although she felt more fetal movement than ever yesterday on November twenty-ninth.' Do you remember relating that to him?"

"I remember slightly," Brenda responded.

For some reason, I could almost predict what Brinkman's next question was going to be. He was just following the records. November thirtieth was the date Dr. Hall sent Brenda to the hospital for a stress test on the fetus because she wasn't feeling movement. He eventually admitted her for more tests and then released her later that night. That was the point when Dr. Hall put Brenda on strict bed rest.

Brinkman continued to follow the records through the first week of December. He asked, "Do you recall on November thirtieth, or within a week thereafter, any further discussions with him as to when the baby would be delivered or the need to have the baby delivered?"

"This is when he kept stressing to make it to the end of, you know, December," Brenda replied. "He said, 'The baby will be full term then. Let's make it to the end of December.'"

"Those were the words he used, 'The baby will be full term then'?" Brinkman asked.

"I'm not sure the exact words on that," Brenda replied.

89

"Well, did you assume that there was some problem that he was trying to get through prior to the baby being delivered?" Brinkman fired back. "Did you ask for anymore explanation?"

Brenda said, "I just remember asking that the baby was okay. I wanted to make sure the baby was okay. And he assured me the baby was okay. But that's again when he really stressed I would go home and have bed rest."

"Do you remember when it was that you went to the hospital?" Brinkman asked. "Was there an occasion when you went to the hospital, before Christmas?"

"Yes," Brenda said. "This was around December twenty-first and was the day I started feeling really bad at my home, when I was on strict bed rest. So I went to see Dr. Russell. He examined me and checked my blood pressure, and he immediately called Dr. Hall."

I couldn't figure Brinkman out. The more Brenda seemed to remember the events leading up to Brett's eventual birth, the faster he wanted to move along with his questions. He asked a few questions about her being induced on December twenty-first and twenty-second. I thought he would ask a thousand questions about these dates. I guess I was wrong.

"Did Dr. Hall come in to the hospital while you were there?" he asked.

"Not on the twenty-first," Brenda responded. "He came in the next evening, on the twenty-second."

"What did Dr. Hall then recommend be done?" Brinkman asked.

"He told me it was against his better judgment, but he would let me go home for Christmas. But he still wanted me to stay in bed," Brenda responded.

"Did you ask him why it was against his better judgment?" Brinkman continued.

"No, I did not," Brenda replied.

"So two efforts to induce labor were on the twenty-first before the holiday, and then you went home and came back on the twenty-seventh, when further efforts were made to induce labor?" Brinkman asked.

"I was induced all that day, as I can remember," Brenda answered.

"What effect did that have?" Brinkman continued.

"I was having contractions, but I might have dilated just a little, but not much at all," Brenda replied.

"And how often was Dr. Hall in to see you on the twenty-seventh?" Brinkman asked.

"I don't believe he came in any that day." Brenda tried to remember. "He showed up later that evening. When I'm saying evening, you know, 5:30 p.m. I don't know for sure, though. It was later in the day. I can remember him telling my husband to go eat supper after he knew he was going to do a C-section, so it was later in the day."

"Okay. At some time he came in that evening, and it was decided he would do a C-section? Did he give you some reason for that?" Brinkman asked.

"He just came in, and we asked what was going on," Brenda recalled. "At this point, we were beginning to worry about our baby being induced so many times and nothing happening."

"What was your basis for believing that? What was your basis for thinking that was likely to happen?"

"I suppose we were just getting scared at that point," Brenda replied.

"What did he say?" Brinkman asked.

"He just said, 'Let's do a C-section,'" Brenda responded.

"Until that conservation, did anybody seeing you there at the hospital mention doing a C-section?" Brinkman asked.

"On the twenty-first, we knew our baby would be born on the

twenty-seventh," Brenda quickly replied.

"Well, you were going to have an induction of labor on the twenty-seventh," Brinkman quickly fired right back.

"Right," Brenda responded. "And I cannot remember if he had mentioned the C-section or not. I just remember us knowing our baby was going to be born on the twenty-seventh."

"Were you told if the induction failed that he would do a C-section? Was that told to you prior to arriving on the twenty-seventh? Did anybody but Dr. Hall mention the C-section to you on the twenty-seventh?"

"Not that I can remember," Brenda said.

Mr. Brinkman continued to ask questions revolving around the C-section. He then moved on to wanting information about what happened to Brett after he was transferred to Children's Memorial Hospital. Brenda explained that she really didn't recall much of that information because she was in and out of the anesthetic. She said, "I can remember my husband coming in and out, saying Brett was having difficulty breathing and that they were transferring him."

It was near this point that I thought Brinkman was about done with his questions for Brenda. He was doing some follow up questions regarding answers she had given earlier in her deposition. I thought Brenda was doing a great job. Little did I know that Brinkman was getting ready to change that feeling.

"Why was it you left Dr. Hall's care eventually?" he asked.

"I did not go back to Dr. Hall after we pursued getting our records investigated," Brenda replied.

"Because you knew that some litigation or claim was being contemplated," Brinkman said. "Did you stop going, do you know, before your attorney requested a copy of his records?"

"Yes, I stopped going to him before my attorney requested the records," Brenda responded.

"And was that because you knew that the record request was

going to be made and some action was at least going to be contemplated?" Brinkman asked.

"I just didn't feel comfortable going back to him," Brenda explained.

"Now, you wrote him a to-whom-it-may-concern letter on April tenth of '84. Do you remember that?"

"Yes, I do," Brenda replied.

"What were the circumstances under which you wrote that letter?" Brinkman asked.

"Dr. Hall called me at home and told me that the hospital was questioning his reason for doing my C-section," Brenda recalled. "He wanted to know if I would write a letter to the hospital stating that I was in agreement with the C-section. He wanted to know if Dr. Russell would also write a letter."

"And the letter that I see here of April tenth of '84 was typed," Brinkman said, looking at his records. "Did you type it?"

"Yes, I did," Brenda replied.

"You concluded the letter by saying, 'We are very grateful to Dr. Hall for agreeing to perform the C-section as the doctors at Children's Memorial said our baby's condition would have worsened should we have waited longer than we did.'"

Up until this point, I just looked straight ahead and listened to the opposing attorney drill Brenda with questions. I thought she was doing a great job. I knew her memory was not as good as mine. The only questions that I thought she might have had problems with were the ones regarding how many times she was induced before Brett was born. Mr. Brinkman's last question took me by surprise. I did not recall any doctor at Children's Memorial telling me that Brett's condition would have worsened if we would have waited any longer than we did. I also thought the letter was from Dr. Russell. I always figured Brenda typed out the letter for him from his office. I knew nothing about a second letter from Brenda to the hospital. I started wondering if this was some kind of trick question. Did the opposing attorney let Brenda get comfortable with his questions, and now he was going in for the kill? I wanted to tell Brenda to say "I don't remember!" Instead, I looked straight ahead and watched our ship slowly sink.

"That's what you said in the letter?" Brinkman asked.

"Apparently that's what I said in the letter," Brenda responded in a low voice.

"And that was accurate and truthful?" Brinkman snapped back.

Brenda looked flustered on how to answer the question. "I don't remember if a doctor or a nurse or who it was at Children's Memorial," Brenda replied. "I don't remember being told that."

"Well, would there have been anyone else to tell you that at the time you typed that letter or prepared that letter?" Brinkman again snapped back.

"Not that I'm aware of," Brenda said.

"Now, who requested Dr. Russell to write the letter?" Brinkman asked. "Did you ask Dr. Russell to write the letter, or did Dr. Hall speak to Dr. Russell? Do you know?"

"Dr. Hall asked me to ask Dr. Russell," Brenda said.

"I see a letter from Dr. Russell of April ninth of '84," Brinkman said. "Let me show you a copy of it. It's a terrible copy. Have you seen that letter before today?"

"Yes," Brenda replied.

"Did you type the letter?" Brinkman asked.

"Probably, but I can't say for sure," Brenda again said in a low voice.

"Who prepared Dr. Russell's letter?" Brinkman asked.

"I don't remember," Brenda responded.

Mr. Brinkman asked several more questions about the letters.

He was beginning to rub it in a little too much. Everyone in the room knew who prepared both letters.

He then started asking questions that had already been answered earlier in the deposition. His questions were jumping back and forth about things already discussed. All of a sudden, he shot out a question that took Brenda and me both by surprise.

Mr. Brinkman stood up from his chair before asking the question. "Did you have any discussions with anybody, either at the hospital, at Children's Memorial, or with Dr. Hall or Dr. Russell, concerning pressure settings on the ventilator that was being used on Brett that may have caused any injury to Brett?"

Brenda just sat there a few moments and then finally answered the question. "I don't remember."

I was sitting there trying to figure out what the hell Brinkman was talking about. No one ever mentioned anything about a faulty ventilator to us. Our attorney never mentioned this.

Mr. Brinkman asked Brenda a few final questions. "I think you already told me, but I want to be sure I understand, that at Children's Memorial Hospital no one told you why the baby was having the problems he was having there?"

"My husband was mostly there. I had had the C-section, and I couldn't get out of the hospital for several days" Brenda replied. "Most of the dealings at Children's Memorial were dealt with by my husband."

"Now, are you aware, and I'll ask your husband this in a minute," Brinkman started. "Has your husband told you that someone provided him with any explanation as to why Brett has cerebral palsy?"

"Not that I'm aware of," Brenda responded.

Mr. Brinkman placed his notepad and pen on the conference table and said, "I don't think I have any further questions. Help me if I missed something."

We stopped to take a short break before my deposition. I could tell Brenda was stressing about some of her answers. I told her to relax and that she did a great job. Getting ambushed with questions about events that happened over ten years earlier is difficult to describe.

I was very surprised with all the questions about the movement, or lack of movement, regarding the fetus on and around November thirtieth. Then there was the question about pressure settings on the ventilator used on Brett the night he was born.

I started to wonder how strong our case actually was. Did Dr. Hall's experts have totally different opinions regarding the cause of Brett's cerebral palsy? A jury would surely be confused at this point if we were in a trial setting. It started to become very clear to me that both sides were digging in for a fight to the end.

CHAPTER 8

During the short break we took between depositions, Brenda and I went down the elevator and stepped outside for some fresh air. We just stood in the sun for a few minutes before going back up to our attorney's office. I told Brenda that I would be right in after I went to the restroom. Just as I was getting ready to go back into the office, I met Mr. Brinkman as he entered the restroom. With a smile, he stopped me and said, "Mr. Meyer, I'm so sorry about the untimely death of your father. You have my deepest sympathy."

Surprised by his kind gesture, all I could say was "Thank you."

Now it was my turn to be deposed. After being sworn in, Mr. Brinkman told me the ground rules that were used in Brenda's deposition would be the same for me. He asked me several questions about my education and occupation. His questions soon got to the point.

"When did you first meet Dr. Hall?" Mr. Brinkman asked.

"I believe the first time was one of Brenda's office visits," I responded.

"Is that when she went to the hospital for testing?" he asked. "Is that the occasion in which she felt that the fetus had stopped moving?"

"Not at that time, no," I answered.

"When did you first learn that she felt that the fetus had stopped moving?" Brinkman continued.

"As I remember, it was around the end of November," I recalled. "I received a message at work that Brenda was at the hospital with her mother for tests and I was supposed to come straight to the hospital after work."

Brinkman asked, "Did you speak to Dr. Hall that day?"

"Yes, I did," I responded.

"What did he say, and what did you say?" he quickly asked.

"He basically said that he was going to put Brenda on bed rest," I answered. "He wanted her to quit work and go on strict bed rest for the duration of the pregnancy."

Mr. Brinkman asked, "Was anything said about the baby as to when it would be delivered and anything about the baby's condition?"

"He had told us previously and then again that day that we needed to make it to the twenty-seventh day of December," I replied. "At that point the baby would be at thirty-seven weeks."

"Why the need to make it?" he asked. "In what context was that said? Was there a problem that was going to be helped to maintain the pregnancy through the end of the year?"

"No," I said. "He told us at thirty-seven weeks the baby would be fully developed. He told us when we arrived at that date he would reevaluate how things were going."

"When was that said, what office visit?" Brinkman fired back.

"It was an office visit I went to with Brenda in November," I said, trying to remember.

"Let's see if I see a November office visit," Brinkman said as he looked at his notes. "November twelfth? I think he shows two office visits: November twelfth, when he did the third ultrasound, and then November thirtieth, when she related the lack of fetal movement."

"It must have been November twelfth," I said. "I'm not sure. But I do remember him doing an ultrasound on Brenda."

"And you were there that day?" he asked. "Were you in the room when it was done?"

"Yes, I was," I responded.

"Were there any problems being related either by her or him on that office visit?" Brinkman asked.

"No, everything was fine," I replied.

Mr. Brinkman looked over his notes for a few moments and

then continued. "And a conversation in his office note says: 'Impression: EDC,' that's the estimated date of the delivery, '1/15/84. Probably consistent with previous ultrasound but difficult to compare because of unavailability of the prenatal chart,' which apparently was out of his office that moment. But is that inconsistent, his writing down that the delivery date was estimated at January fifteenth of '84, with you telling me that he said that by the end of December the baby would be mature?"

Our attorney Ms. Dunkin quickly jumped in and asked, "Do you understand the question?"

"I think I do," I responded. "He took us into his office after the ultrasound and told us everything looked great. I don't remember how many weeks he said the baby was at that point, but he then looked at his calendar and said we needed to make it to December twenty-seventh. He told us the twenty-seventh was an important date. He also said once we reached that point, he would have to make a decision whether to let the pregnancy continue or end it."

Brinkman seemed flustered with my answerers. I felt like he was digging for some particular answer or information. "Why was that an important date?" He continued, "Did you know or did he tell you?"

"Because he said the baby would be fully developed at that point," I answered.

"Any questions about Brenda's high blood pressure?" Brinkman asked.

"We all knew she had high blood pressure," I replied. "There was no problem at that point, no."

"Any discussion about her having been on Corgard?" he asked.

"No," I replied.

"On your wife's—" he said, and then he stopped himself. "Well, you were not married to your wife when she had her first baby. Did anybody inquire of him on that November office visit why you just weren't going to wait until she had contractions and went into labor, regardless of whether it was December twenty-seventh or January third or any other date?"

I now had too many dates starting to go through my head. If Brinkman was trying to confuse me, he was doing a great job. I finally asked him if he would repeat the question.

"I don't quite understand the context of his explaining that December twenty-seventh was an important date," Brinkman replied. "Did you ask him why it was important?"

"As I remember, he told us," I answered. "He told us when any of his patients, when a woman was in her thirty-seventh week, or when she went into labor in her thirty-seventh week, he did not stop her because the baby would be, is always, fully developed at that time. And in Brenda's case, to reach that point would be the twenty-seventh of December."

Mr. Brinkman seemed as confused as I was. "Okay," he said. "I guess I'm trying to find out whether the context of that was that your wife is having problems or potential problems and we hope to get her through December twenty-seventh, or by December twenty-seventh the baby will be fully developed and whenever it is born thereafter is okay. Is it one or the other of those scenarios?"

"I'm sorry," I replied. "Apparently I'm not understanding the question."

Brinkman rephrased the question. "The fact that he mentioned December twenty-seventh was in no way stated by him to be in reference to any problem that your wife was having?"

"No," I finally answered.

"And he repeated the same thing after the November thirtieth visit you told me?" he asked.

"Yes, that's correct," I replied.

Brinkman finally moved on from asking any further questions about November thirtieth. He switched focus to December twenty-first. He asked a few questions about whether I had any conversations with Dr. Hall leading up to that particular date. I told him there were no conversations.

"Do you know why he was inducing labor on December twenty-first?" Brinkman asked.

"I remember Brenda was not feeling well on that day," I recalled. "I received a message at work to come home immediately. When I arrived home, Brenda told me we needed to get to the hospital. Dr. Hall had said it was time for the baby to be born."

Brinkman asked, "What conversation did you have with Dr. Hall during the hospitalization on the twenty-first?"

"I don't remember seeing him on the twenty-first," I responded. "We didn't arrive at the hospital until later that evening."

He asked, "She stayed overnight until the twenty-second?"

"Yes, she did," I said.

"And what was said about why she was in or the condition of your wife or the baby?"

"He said he was going to let us go home for the holidays even though it was against his medical judgment," I responded.

"What did he mean by that?" Brinkman quickly asked.

"I have no idea," I replied.

"Did you ask him?" Brinkman fired back.

"I asked him if everything was all right, and he assured me it was," I quickly replied.

Brinkman asked, "What was your impression as to why she was being induced on the twenty-first or twenty-second?"

"Because he told us it was time for the baby to be born, and he didn't want to continue the pregnancy," I replied.

Mr. Brinkman asked, "Did he tell you why?"

"Because he thought the baby was fully developed and he

didn't... She was starting to feel bad as far as the headaches, and he said it was time to go ahead and deliver the baby," I answered.

Brinkman asked, "So this had to do with some complaints that your wife had?"

I responded, "Just that one day. The day before."

"Okay," Brinkman said. "So when you went home and when you left that day, your wife said you went out and celebrated at Red Lobster. Do you remember that?"

When Brinkman asked the question, I sat there a few seconds wondering how to answer. I knew Brenda and I stopped off to eat on our way to the hospital, not on the way home. I didn't want to make Brenda look bad, so I compromised and said, "I do remember a time when we celebrated at Red Lobster before the baby was born, yes."

Brinkman asked, "And do you agree with her testimony about at that time you knew the baby was going to be born on the twenty-seventh?"

Again I compromised and said, "I remember celebrating because we knew we would have a baby on the twenty-seventh, yes."

"What did Dr. Hall tell you about that, if he told you anything?" Brinkman asked. "Did he tell you about what was going to happen on the twenty-eighth?"

I responded, "He said that he would induce her the twenty-seventh, and we would take it from there."

Brinkman asked, "Were you with her when she went in on the twenty-seventh?"

"Yes, I was," I answered.

"And did you have any conversations that day with Dr. Hall?" Brinkman asked.

"He was not there all day until that evening," I responded.

Brinkman asked, "What was said that evening?"

"We questioned him about what was going on as far as why this was the third day that she had been induced, and we were concerned," I explained. "We asked him if there was something wrong, why, you know, what he was going to do, if he was going to, what his plans were. And he planned... He said, we will I guess induce tomorrow, and then he mentioned the C-section."

"What did he say about that?" Brinkman asked.

"All I can remember is him saying is 'Fine, let's just do a C-section,'" I responded.

Mr. Brinkman asked, "Was that an option presented, further induction tomorrow or a C-section, with his recommending the C-section?"

"He had mentioned it, but then he said 'Let's just do a C-section,'" I explained.

Brinkman asked, "Did he ask you to leave that decision up to you or your wife whether to do the C-section?"

"I presume he addressed both of us when he mentioned that," I recalled. "We were both there."

"Was it your understanding that you and your wife had a decision to make as to whether to have the C-section or induce labor, or merely that this was what he was recommending and you agreed to it?" Brinkman asked.

I answered, "It's basically what he recommended."

Mr. Brinkman asked, "Did you and your wife discuss the C-section before he spoke about it?"

"No, we hadn't," I responded.

"You said about the third day about induction," Brinkman started. "Were the first two days the twenty-first and twenty-second?"

I replied, "Yes."

Mr. Brinkman said, "So, at first he came in. You said you all were concerned and questioned him whether something was wrong, and he said that he guessed he would have another day of induction tomorrow but finally said let's go ahead and do a C-section?"

I responded, "Yes, he did."

Brinkman asked, "Did you have any conversations with him after the C-section? In specific, I guess I should relate it to either how the C-section went or the cause of Brett's condition."

"I think, as I remember, he told me that Brenda was in recovery and was doing fine," I responded.

He asked, "What did he say about the baby initially?"

"At the time, nothing was mentioned," I replied.

"Anybody up there at the hospital with you that day, other than you and Brenda? Any family members?" Brinkman asked.

"No," I answered.

Mr. Brinkman asked, "Were you getting any input or recommendations from any other healthcare personnel at the hospital? Were any other doctors or nurses up there making recommendations to you?"

"As far as Brenda was concerned, no," I answered.

Brinkman then asked, "What about as far as Brett?"

I asked, "After he was born?"

"Yes," Mr. Brinkman responded.

I said, "There was I guess the house pediatrician that talked to me."

"Who was that who was taking charge of Brett's care after his birth?" Brinkman asked.

"Dr. Dawson initially came in later that night," I answered.

Mr. Brinkman asked, "Was he a family pediatrician?"

"It's a she," I said.

Brinkman looked at me with a confused look and said, "She?"

"Yes. She arrived later that evening," I replied.

"Had she taken care of Gina?" he asked.

"No," I responded.

Brinkman then asked, "How did you get Dr. Dawson?"

"I have no idea," I answered.

Brinkman kind of smiled and said, "Okay. Let me ask you first about Dr. Hall, whether he has ever made any comments, either to you or that you overheard, concerning the cause of Brett's condition?"

"He has not, no," I responded.

Mr. Brinkman asked, "Have you ever asked him for any explanation?"

"No," I replied.

"Has anyone made statements as to why Brett has had the problems he has had?"

"As far as I know nobody has ever made any statements as to the cause," I responded.

"Has Dr. Hall made any comments that you overheard in which he has accepted or admitted any liability or fault in treating your wife?" Brinkman asked.

"No," I responded.

Mr. Brinkman then asked, "You were here when I questioned your wife and when Ms. Dunkin questioned her about... I think your wife mentioned something about a hemorrhage due to his prematurity. Did anyone tell you that Brett had a hemorrhage due to prematurity?"

"Not that I'm aware of," I answered.

Brinkman quickly asked, "Aren't you asking at Children's Memorial what's going on here?"

"Yes, I was," I said.

Brinkman fired back, "And what were you told?"

"As far as when I admitted him at Children's Memorial early that morning, basically they just told me that he was... Due to his prematurity, they needed to get him back into his own environment, which basically was the incubator," I replied.

Now I really had Brinkman confused. He asked, "Was the what? Ventilator?"

"No," I said. "I'm sorry. When I say incubator, it was the enclosed bed. The bed was enclosed in glass with little holes in the side to put your hands through."

"All right," Brinkman said. "What about Dr. Dawson? Did she follow the baby down at Children's Memorial?"

"No, she didn't," I replied.

Brinkman asked, "Is there anything that you, in listening to your wife describe Brett's present functioning and condition, anything that you can remember wanting to add to that so that I can understand what his condition is now?"

"I think the only thing that wasn't mentioned is he is dependent on us for bathing, and that's getting to be a real problem," I responded.

Mr. Brinkman asked, "What does he weigh now?"

"I would say... I would estimate around fifty-five pounds," I replied. "But it's the length of his body now that kind of makes it difficult to lift him in and out of the tub."

Mr. Brinkman said, "I don't think I have any other questions."

CHAPTER 9

With our depositions finally behind us, it was time to try and get back into a normal routine again. Between my dad's accidental death and the time spent giving our depositions, Brenda and I had missed several days of work in the past weeks. We were both mentally exhausted.

Both kids were already settled in to a new school year. Gina was turning into a very beautiful young lady, and the boys were starting to take notice. I couldn't believe that in just over a year she would be eligible for a driving permit. She was growing up so fast. She already had a job working on weekends at the local pizza restaurant. Brenda and I were very proud of her.

Brett was making great progress walking short distances unassisted with a walker. Even though he had made great progress in building up his legs, we were getting increasingly concerned about his posture while seated in his wheelchair. For some reason, he constantly needed to be reminded to sit up in his chair, and within minutes he would be slumped over again. Dr. Williams, his orthopedic specialist, told us that we would have to address the issue in the years ahead. I didn't understand the meaning of that statement, but at that point I wasn't prepared to take on any more complications in our life.

My mother was doing as well as could be expected. She was having good and bad days as time passed. It made me feel better knowing my brother was living under the same roof and they both had each other to lean on. It was so hard watching my mother grieve for the love of her life. I knew in time she would be fine because she was a very strong woman.

My brother was also having a hard time dealing with the death of our father. He was blaming himself for what happened on that tragic day. My dad was climbing a ladder to the roof they had built the day before when the mishap happened. Just as he started to step on the upper roof, the aluminum ladder he was on slipped, causing him to lose his balance. Somehow in the process of falling from the upper roof to the lower roof and then rolling off to the ground, he sustained the injury that led to his ultimate demise.

I can only imagine what my brother went through trying to help Dad after the accident happened. Gary was right at his side when he hit the ground. Dad told my brother he was okay. Gary helped him to his feet and assisted him, trying to get him back to the house. About halfway there, Dad went to the ground. That's when my brother called nine-one-one. My brother did everything he could do. He had no reason to feel any different.

Everyone around me was going through such great emotions. My dad's death left me empty and numb inside. He was the one person I could unload my frustrations about work or other problems to, and he would always guide me to a positive direction. I knew God had a plan for us, but I was having a hard time figuring out how I fit into the plan. My only hope was that I would have the strength to face what was ahead without my father's guidance.

Financially my mother was in great shape. My parents' investments over the years left them with a nice nest egg. My dad also left behind a small life insurance policy and an accidental death policy, which added to the estate. The only assets that would need to go through probate were corporate shares in my father's name that were inherited after the death of my grandmother. She went through a long battle with cancer and passed away just days before Brenda and I got married. It was very bittersweet for my family enduring a funeral and wedding all in the same week. The corporate shares that needed to go through probate court were part of the family farming operation. It was all very confusing. I had no choice but to figure the whole situation out on my own to protect my mother's future interests in these shares.

My next concern was my brother. I started pumping him for information about what was going on with his health. It was really hard to get anything out of him. He was going two and three times a week for overnight treatments at the hospital. They were using ultraviolet light on his blood and whole body. Somehow his blood was being pumped through a machine that treated it with the ultraviolet light. Other times, he would stand in a chamber and expose his entire body to ultraviolet light. The effects were devastating. Some days he would come to work looking like he had walked through the desert sun for days without any protection, and the days after he would be shedding skin like a snake. Most days he just looked miserable with the dry, itchy skin. One night, he took his work boot and sock off on our drive home. I swear the bottom of his foot had cracks that were at least a half-inch deep. I don't know how he had the strength to get up and go to work each day. I felt bad because I wanted him to get laid off work so he could rest his body.

I finally asked my brother if he would let me talk to his doctor about his condition. His response was "My doctor was wondering if I even had a family. She's been treating me for over a year now, and she has never met or talked with anyone about my condition."

His answer took me by surprise. I sensed a little anger in his voice, and I knew I was on thin ice. I didn't want to say something that would make him clam up and not talk. I finally said, "Gary, we are really concerned about you. Please open up and let us help you. You tell us everything is all right, but it clearly isn't. Please let us help you. We need to know what is going on."

He finally opened up a little bit. He was going to have the doctor call me. I told him my concerns about how work was wearing on his body. He explained that between child support and an enormous amount of credit card debt, he had no choice but to continue to work as long as possible. I told him we needed to discuss this subject again during the next appointment with our attorney when we finalized our father's estate. He agreed it was time to do something.

I finally talked to my brother's doctor a few days later. She was very direct in our conversation about my brother. She told me that his condition was very serious. Her main concern was the chance of the malignancy moving to other parts of his body. I think I asked the doctor three different times if his condition was treatable. Her response was that they were doing everything possible to contain the malignancy.

After talking with the doctor, a very sick feeling rushed through my body. It was the same feeling I had the night Brett was born. Why was it so hard for me to connect the dots regarding my brother's condition? Was I so obsessed with my own family problems that I didn't bother thinking about what was really going on with my only brother. The malignancy was not just a spot on his body. It was not a skin cancer or melanoma. My brother had cancer of the skin. The whole entire outer shell of his body was infested with cancer. All the treatments he had been putting his body through were actually experimental. There was no cure for his condition.

Just like the night Brenda told me Brett had cerebral palsy, I again went into denial. I started coming up with other explanations for his condition. Even though I knew I was wrong, it comforted me that my brother was finally letting me get involved.

In the middle of October, I was working downtown, constructing a new parking garage. The job was just starting, so I figured it was my home for the winter. It had been awhile since I last worked outside in the elements. Pouring concrete and packing materials through the mud were starting to wear on my body for the first time in my life. With winter approaching, the days were starting to get shorter. It was dark when I went to work and when I arrived home in the evening.

On a normal day, I usually picked up Brett on my way home from work. The school bus would drop him off at the Catholic school in town, which provided after-school care. I usually picked him up by five o' clock, and we would go home and start supper. Gina was normally home already working on her homework.

One particular day was much different from all the others as I arrived to pick Brett up. I walked down the steps to the lower level of the school where I knew Brett would be. When I walked through the doorway, I could see him at the other end of the room. As I walked towards him, I couldn't believe what I was looking at. I remember saying, "What the hell!"

As I approached him, I heard a voice say, "That didn't happen here!"

Brett's white shirt was covered with blood.

When I asked him what happened, he said, "It wasn't my fault!"

The lady from the after-school care told me she was shocked when she went to get Brett off the bus. She said, "I asked the bus driver what happened. He told me Brett was like this when they brought him to the bus."

Brett had an inch-long gash on his forehead between his eyes. He also had a nasty bruise that was one-inch wide. It started just below his ear and extended down his neck to his throat. I immediately rushed him to where Brenda worked to see Doc before the clinic closed.

Doc said the cut probably should have been stitched, but it was too late. He dressed the cut with butterfly strips. Brenda went into Brett's backpack to see if there was a note from his school explaining what had happened. When she opened up the daily log notebook, there was a notation from his teacher." Brett had an accident with the floor today... The floor won."

If someone had handed me a phone book at that point, I would have ripped it in half. Why did we not get a call from the school regarding this accident? Why didn't someone call Brenda and say Brett had a little mishap, that he might need stitches? I wonder what would have happened if we sent Brett to school in the same condition with the same explanation. We would have been in jail.

Every morning, I told myself today was going to be a better day, and then every evening a new problem or mishap like this one would arise. I was beginning to lose my patience with the school district. We contacted the principal of the school the next day. He assured us he would do a thorough investigation. The investigation must have ended as soon as he put the phone down. There was never another word mentioned about the incident.

We were already in the month of November, and I was looking forward to the approaching three-day weekend because of Veterans Day. I had several things I wanted to do that I normally couldn't get done during the work week.

Friday afternoon, I started having severe pain in my left shoulder on my drive home. It felt like someone had shot me with gun. I couldn't understand what I did to it to make it hurt so bad. The pain continued off and on through the whole weekend, so Brenda made me come into the office that Monday morning to have Doc look at it. He couldn't find anything structurally wrong after examining me, so he put me on some muscle relaxers and said we would see if it helped.

When I went to work on Tuesday, I told my boss about my weekend. I asked if I should fill out an accident report about my shoulder. He asked me what happened, and I told him the pain started when I got in my truck to drive home. He told me I couldn't fill out an injury report if I didn't know how I was injured.

"My shoulder was fine when I started work on Friday morning and hurt like hell when I left to go home," I replied.

My boss again said, "Until you tell me how you injured your shoulder, I'm not filling out a report."

At first, the muscle relaxers seemed to be working, but by the end of the week the discomfort was back again. Everything I was doing at work seemed to aggravate the situation. I constantly had to look up and reach up to land materials with a tower crane, which is used on major construction projects, especially high-rise buildings, to hoist essential materials to supply a job site. By the time Thanksgiving arrived, I was in misery. After spending Thanksgiving Day with family, the pain started to get out of hand that evening. It was getting so bad that it started moving down my arm into the elbow. My fingers were even tingling. Brenda finally had enough. She said, "I'm taking you to the hospital." At that point I didn't care. I needed something to relieve the pain. Gina said her and Brett would be fine.

When I got to the ER, the first thing they wanted were X-rays of my shoulder, which of course showed nothing. The doctor then gave me a shot of Toradol to help ease the pain. He then suggested a cortisone shot into the shoulder joint. I was willing to try anything. He told me if I didn't see any improvement by Monday that I should be seen by an orthopedic specialist.   On Monday I was still having discomfort, so Brenda had Doc call to see if he could get me in with someone that day. He called me back and told me to head to the hospital. He said the orthopedic doctor would try to look at my shoulder between surgeries. I was supposed to wait for him in the surgical waiting area. When he came to see me, he took me into hallway and asked what was going on. After telling him what had gone on for the last several weeks, he asked if I could come back later that afternoon for an MRI. I agreed to come back. He told me to wait and that his nurse would be out shortly to tell me what time to come back for the MRI on my neck.

I said, "You mean shoulder."

"No," he replied." I want the MRI on your neck. I believe you have a disk in your neck that is causing the discomfort in your shoulder."

This took me by complete surprise. After thinking about it driving home, it started making sense why I couldn't figure out what I did to my shoulder. My boss was going to freak out because we never filed an incident report. Luckily for me I didn't lie and dream up something I did to injure my shoulder. I also started wondering if I was going to need surgery, or if I was going to miss a substantial amount of work time. I was soon going to get my answer, but it would be in a very surprising way.

I arrived back at the hospital around four that afternoon for the MRI. The whole process seemed simple enough. I had no problem being put into a small tube and staying still for the forty-five minutes that the test took. Everything went great until the end. When the test was over, the guy pulled me out of the tube and removed some cushions he had placed under my knees. He told me I could go ahead and sit up while he was filling out papers at a counter just to my right. I looked at the counter to my left and could see my wallet, watch, and keys. I asked the guy if I could get my personal articles. Without looking at me, he said sure.

In the next two to five seconds, several things were going to happen out of my control. When I looked down to jump off the table, my feet were probably sixteen inches off the floor. When both feet hit the floor, I immediately knew something wasn't right. I guess the pillows placed under my knees during the MRI cut the circulation off to both of my lower legs because I first watched my left ankle completely roll over then watched the right foot do the same. As I started to fall forward, somehow I did a complete flip and crashed into some equipment next to the door. When I looked down at my legs, the feeling suddenly returned to my lower extremities. The pain was unbelievable. The MRI attendant rushed to me screaming, "What happened?"

"My feet must have been asleep!" I yelled. "I think both my ankles are broke!"

As I lay there screaming in pain, the door suddenly opened. A nurse was bringing in an elderly gentleman in a wheelchair for his own MRI. I will never forget the face on the poor old guy as he watched me roll in pain on the floor. His eyes were as big as silver dollars! They finally called for help and rushed me to the ER. I asked to use a phone to call Brenda at work. One of the nurses at the office answered and said Brenda would be with me in just a minute. When she came on the phone, she immediately asked how the MRI went. I told her the MRI went great but I had an accident getting off the MRI table. "I think both my ankles are broke. They're getting ready to take me for X-rays."

At first there was a long pause, and then she asked, "You are kidding, aren't you?"

"I wish I was. I feel like an idiot."

Brenda asked what had happened, but I told her I needed to hang up because they were taking me for X-rays.

Brenda arrived at the hospital about the time the orthopedic surgeon walked into my room. He looked at me and said, "Keith, you've had a heck of a day."

"No kidding," I said.

He continued to tell me that he had good news and bad news. The good news was there was no visible damage to either ankle on the X-rays, but both were severely sprained.

"The bad news is the MRI did indicate a bulging disk in your neck. I suggest once you're back on your feet enough to come back to the hospital that we try some steroid injections into your neck to shrink the inflammation. You're allowed up to three injections. If that doesn't work, we will have to consider surgery as a last resort." He then told me he didn't want me returning to work until everything was healed up completely.

Surprisingly it took longer for my ankles to heal versus my

neck. I ended up taking two injections into my neck before the discomfort was gone. I knew it could return at any time, but at least for now I had relief. It took three weeks for my ankles to heal enough for me to return to work. My company was happy because it was not considered a lost time incident since the majority of the lost time came from the accident at the hospital.

CHAPTER 10

It was time for the doctor's deposition. This time our attorney would be asking the questions. I was really starting to stress over how much money was being spent by our representation regarding this case. Every month our account balance was jumping several thousand dollars at a time. I was to the point where I actually wondered if a jury awarded Brett fifty thousand dollars if it would actually cover the legal bills. I thought Brenda and I could have done much better with our depositions, but it was too late to worry about it. At that point I figured if our case went before a jury it would be a crapshoot. I was really interested how the doctor would handle his deposition. Because the doctor had moved to a different state, his deposition had been rescheduled several times. They finally agreed on a date over Thanksgiving weekend. He was deposed on the Friday after Thanksgiving at our attorney's office. Dr. Hall was accompanied by his attorney, Mr. Brinkman. Here is how his deposition unfolded:

"Did you bring any particular records with you that you have maintained over the years on this particular case?" Mr. Stone asked.

"No, sir, I'm sorry, I did not." Dr. Hall answered.

"Now, you know that I am the attorney for the plaintiff in this case, and my name is Jim Stone. I'm going to be asking you questions about the care and treatment that you rendered to Brenda Meyer in her pregnancy and delivery with Brett Meyer. If I should ask you something that you don't understand, or you don't hear me, or for any reason you have a question about the question, I will ask you to tell me about it before you attempt to answer. Can we agree on that, that you will do that?"

Dr. Hall replied, "Yes, sir."

"Very good. Would you tell me what periventricular leukomalacia is?" Mr. Stone asked.

"I'm not really sure," Hall replied.

"Do you have some general idea?" Stone asked.

Dr. Hall responded, "Only in the broadest sense that it is some sort of defect in the brain."

"Do you know if it has anything to do with hemorrhaging within the brain?" Mr. Stone asked.

Hall replied, "I do not know."

"Do you know what the causes, the possible causes, are of periventricular leukomalacia?" Stone asked.

Dr. Hall said, "No, I do not."

"Do you know if periventricular leukomalacia can cause cerebral palsy?" Mr. Stone continued.

"I do not know that," Hall responded.

"Can you tell me what the various risks are to an infant of prematurity?" Stone continued. "Can you give me whatever number of risks you can recall for prematurity?"

Mr. Brinkman, Dr. Hall's attorney, quickly jumped in. "Let me object to the question. Before what week? Or can you be more specific because there are a lot of questions about 'What is premature?'"

Mr. Stone responded, "That's true. There are different risks at more serious stages of prematurity, I take it?"

"I was referring to whether you are talking about prematurity by age or by weight, just so we know exactly what you were looking for," Brinkman quickly responded.

"I'm specifically speaking about age, gestational age, premature gestational age," Mr. Stone replied. "Let's start by identifying what you, as an obstetrician, generally consider to be a full-term baby in terms of gestational age."

"A full-term gestation is a gestation that exists from thirty-seven to forty weeks as calculated from the last menstrual period," Dr. Hall responded.

"Thirty-seven to forty weeks?" Stone asked.

Hall replied, "Yes, sir."

"Now, just for the sake of clarity, when we say gestational age, what does that refer to? What does that mean, that term?" Stone then asked.

"That means the length of time that has passed from the first day of the last period to the date, to the present time you are discussing," Hall replied.

"So if we are talking about measuring from a full-term baby, for example, that would be from the first day of the last menstrual period to the birth of the baby? If we are looking at it at the time of birth, that would be the gestational age, right?" Mr. Stone asked.

Dr. Hall said, "I'm sorry, I don't understand the question."

Mr. Stone rephrased his question to Dr. Hall. "On the day of the baby's birth, if we are talking about his gestational age, we are talking about the time from the last menstrual period of his mother until the day he was born?"

Hall answered, "Yes, sir."

"What are the risks of gestational age prematurity between thirty-five and thirty-seven weeks?" Stone asked.

"The risks between thirty-five and thirty-seven weeks are minimal," Hall replied. "They may include the inability of the infant to maintain its temperature, they may include immaturity of the infant's liver so as to not allow the infant to prevent its own jaundice from occurring, and it may include what might be called transient tachypnea, which is, for lack of a better word, a temporary inability to breathe well."

Mr. Brinkman again stepped in on the questioning. "Let me add something that I think you will agree to, Jim. We are talking about babies normal in weight and everything else normal, except the gestational age?"

Mr. Stone said, "Yes"

Mr. Brinkman then added to his point. "Okay. Because you can always hypothesize abnormalities."

Mr. Stone again rephrased his question. "What are the primary risks of gestational age prematurity for babies born at thirty-four weeks of gestational age?"

Dr. Hall responded, "They would include the same three we just mentioned, but also it may include respiratory distress syndrome, but rarely."

Stone then asked, "What is respiratory distress syndrome?"

"Respiratory distress syndrome is the recognized set of signs that an infant would exhibit if it did not have mature lungs," Hall answered.

"I gather that you're telling me that respiratory distress syndrome is the description of what happens to the infant when its lungs are immature, when it's born with immature lungs?" Stone continued.

Dr. Hall responded with, "That's not the only cause of respiratory distress syndrome. You might also see respiratory distress syndrome in an infant that aspirates meconium or has other difficulties that block its lungs for whatever reason."

Mr. Stone asked, "Meconium aspiration is another cause?"

"Meconium aspiration or pneumonia would be another cause," Hall answered.

"Now would you tell me the symptoms of respiratory distress syndrome?" Stone asked.

Dr. Hall responded, "It's difficult for me to do that since I don't care for infants."

"So you are not sure what all the constellation of symptoms would be?" Stone asked.

"Correct," Hall replied.

"Now, you say that at thirty-four weeks a child would be at risk for, a new born would be at risk for, the same three problems that you mentioned at thirty-five to thirty-seven weeks, plus respiratory distress syndrome rarely," Stone continued. "Are there any other risks you can think of for prematurity at thirty-four weeks gestation, premature birth thirty-four weeks gestation?"

"Not at this time," Dr. Hall responded.

"Let's move down to thirty-three weeks of gestation," Stone said. "What are the risks of premature birth at thirty-three weeks gestation? And again, as Mr. Brinkman suggested, remember that we are looking now only at the length of time of gestation, excluding all other problems that might occur."

Mr. Brinkman again stopped the proceedings. "I would object. I'll let him answer, but I'll object that I wonder if you can hypothesize a situation where you would terminate the pregnancy at thirty-three weeks to determine respiratory distress syndrome without there being some other underlying pathology, but subject to that you can answer."

Mr. Stone's response to the objection was, "I'm not asking if he would terminate the pregnancy. I'm just saying if, for one reason or another, a child is born at thirty-three weeks of gestation, what would be the risk because of the gestational period?"

"I would say the four," Hall responded. "The same four items that we have previously listed, but there may be more and I can't answer that because I'm not a neonatologist or a pediatrician."

Stone said, "I'm going to ask the same question now, but instead of thirty-three weeks, we will refer to thirty-two weeks of gestation. What are the risks that a child born at thirty-two weeks of gestation would be subject to?"

"I would have to give the same answer I gave for the thirty-three weeks gestation question," Hall answered.

"From what you know about Brett Meyer, were you aware before this lawsuit whether or not he had periventricular leukomalacia?" Mr. Stone asked.

"No, sir, I was not aware," Dr. Hall responded.

"Were you aware before this lawsuit of whether or not Brett Meyer had cerebral palsy?" Stone then asked.

"Yes, I was aware of that," Hall replied.

"How did you become aware that he had cerebral palsy?" Stone asked.

"Brenda Meyer told me he did," Hall said.

"Were you given any medical information, medical records, that reflected that?" Mr. Stone asked.

Dr. Hall replied, "No, sir."

"Were you consulted by any other physician that was involved in his treatment?" Mr. Stone then asked.

Hall again replied, "No."

"Was your only knowledge of his condition of cerebral palsy by way of Brenda's report?" Stone continued.

"Yes, sir," Hall answered.

"It's true, is it not, that you were Brenda's obstetrician for her pregnancy with Brett?" Stone asked.

Dr. Hall responded, "Yes, sir."

"And is it true you delivered Brett?" Mr. Stone asked.

Dr. Hall again said, "Yes, sir."

"Can you describe for me the events that occurred during the procedure?" Stone asked. "By that I mean was there anything, any particular difficulty with the procedure, any complications encountered, anything out of the ordinary that happened during the cesarean section?"

"I can recall with the aid of the operative note, but not from my recollection," Dr. Hall replied.

Mr. Stone said, "You may look at it if you like."

Dr. Hall replied, "What I recognize from what I dictated was that there was difficulty in entering the amniotic sac and that Brenda lost approximately 1,000 cc's of blood. That was the estimate by the nurse anesthetist. We always allow them to make the estimate of blood loss."

"Does that sort of blood loss require a transfusion?" Stone asked.

Hall responded, "It depends a lot on the case. These days, no. Ten years ago, frequently, yes."

"Was the transfusion resorted to in Brenda's case?" Stone asked.

"I believe one unit of blood was given," Hall replied.

"Will you tell us, in general terms just in case there is someone listening to this testimony that doesn't understand, what is a cesarean section?" Mr. Stone then asked.

"A cesarean section is a major surgery in which the maternal abdomen is entered either vertically or transversely through the skin, and then the incisions are carried out down the peritoneal cavity and an incision is made into the uterus itself," Dr. Hall explained. "And then the infant is delivered manually through the incision, and then the cord, the umbilical cord, is separated. And then the placenta is manually removed, and then all the incisions and openings that were created are then repaired."

"What is persistent fetal circulation?" Stone asked.

Dr. Hall said, "I really don't feel qualified to answer that."

"Do you have a general sense of what it means?" Mr. Stone asked.

Dr. Hall responded, "In a general sense it is the circulation of the fetal blood that does not allow as much oxygenation through the lungs. It allows blood flow away from the lungs because that is the blood flow the fetus has until it's on its own and starts breathing."

"Are you aware of any classical list of causes for persistent fetal circulation?" Stone asked.

"No, sir, I'm not."

Mr. Stone said, "Now, just to clarify, is this a condition that is described in newborn infants?"

"I'm not sure," Dr. Hall replied.

"I mean when they're fetuses, they are supposed to have fetal circulation. Is that a fair statement?" Stone asked.

Hall responded, "Yes, sir."

"And once they are born, their circulatory pattern is supposed to switch over to that of a viable living individual?" Stone continued.

Dr. Hall again said, "Yes, sir."

"And the term as I understand it, and I'm asking you whether my understanding is correct or not, when we talk about persistent fetal circulation, we are describing an abnormality in a neonate, some child who has been born and isn't switching over to the right kind of circulation in a timely fashion?"

"I would think so, yes, sir, but I don't know if there is more to the definition," Hall replied.

Mr. Stone then asked, "What is cerebral palsy?"

"That's a good question," Hall replied. "I can't give you a very inclusive definition. I can give you my understanding of it, not as a pediatrician, but again as an individual. That is a condition in which brain damage exists in one form or another for causes that I do not know and results in the lack of motor skills in the affected individual."

"Is it your understanding that only motor skills are affected?" Stone asked.

Hall replied, "That has been my understanding, yes, sir."

"And when we say motor skills, we are talking about those skills that enable a person to move his limbs and fingers and toes, et cetera, and maybe his head, or just generally move the voluntary muscles of the body?" Mr. Stone asked.

"Yes, sir," Hall answered.

Stone asked, "Is it your understanding, or do you have an understanding, of whether or not that condition of cerebral palsy is a permanent condition?"

"I'm not sure," Hall said.

"Do you have an understanding as to whether or not it is a progressive condition?" Mr. Stone asked. "By that I mean that it is a condition which gets worse as time goes on, either at a slower or faster rate."

"My understanding was that it was not progressive," Dr. Hall answered.

"Do you know whether cerebral palsy has a statistical effect on lifespan, the lifespan of the individuals who are affected with it?" Stone asked.

"I do not know," Hall said.

"You had earlier said that you are not aware of the causes of cerebral palsy," Stone said. "Are you aware of any causes?"

"No, sir, not really," Hall replied.

"You testified earlier that you are not aware of whether or not periventricular leukomalacia can cause it, is that correct?" Mr. Stone asked.

Hall said, "That's what I testified, yes, sir."

"Are you aware of any cause or indication that existed in either Brett Meyer as a fetus or in Brenda Meyer as his mother that was a predictor for either cerebral palsy or any other kind of fetal impairment, or impairment of the child, I should say?" Mr. Stone asked.

Dr. Hall replied, "I'm sorry, I don't understand the question."

"Let's limit it to cerebral palsy," Mr. Stone said. "Are you aware of any other possible causes based upon evidence that existed in either Brenda's medical history or in the fetus' condition during pregnancy that would have been a predictor, or possible predictor, or risk factor for cerebral palsy?"

"It's difficult to answer because I couldn't answer your other questions," Dr. Hall responded.

"What is hyaline membrane disease?" Stone asked.

Dr. Hall said, "Again, it's difficult for me to give you a textbook answer, but I can give you my understanding of it, which I will do. Hyaline membrane disease, in a broad sense—and, again, in the broadest sense—is probably the same thing as respiratory distress syndrome."

"Is prematurity a cause, one of the causes, of respiratory distress syndrome?" Mr. Stone asked.

Hall answered, "Yes, sir."

"And is one of the causes of hyaline membrane disease prematurity?" Stone asked.

Hall replied, "Yes, sir. If it's not a cause, it's an association."

"Do you have an opinion about whether or not prematurity is a cause or just a statistical association with either respiratory distress syndrome—well, take respiratory distress syndrome separately," Stone said. "Do you have an opinion as a physician about that?"

Once again, Mr. Brinkman stopped the proceedings. "I think he already answered the question as he said he thinks hyaline is the same. I think he answered that previously, but you can answer that again."

Mr. Stone said, "I'm only separating the two because first you said they were essentially the same, and then you said hyaline membrane disease is a cause of respiratory distress syndrome. So I'm separating the two. And then we got to the point of whether prematurity causes either one or both of those conditions, and you said, 'Yes, it's a cause or a statistical association.' And now my question is, with respect to each of those conditions separately—respiratory distress syndrome first—do you have an opinion as a physician as to whether prematurity is a cause or merely a statistical association with respiratory distress syndrome?"

"Again, I think the cause is not prematurity," Dr. Hall responded. "I think prematurity is an association with respiratory distress syndrome and with hyaline membrane disease."

"Do you know anything about the physiology of hyaline membrane disease? What does it mean?" Stone asked.

"Hyaline is a component that is recognized in the biochemistry of the body, and if there is not a sufficient quantity of a substance called surfactant, then hyaline membrane disease may exist," Dr. Hall explained.

"And that is a chemical substance produced by the body?" Stone continued.

Hall answered, "Yes, sir."

Mr. Stone asked, "With reference to Brett Meyer in particular, do you have an opinion as the obstetrician who handled the pregnancy and delivery—pregnancy of the mother and delivery of the baby—as to whether or not Brett Meyer was premature?"

"My opinion was he was not premature, except by perhaps one day," Hall replied.

"What did you believe that his gestational age was at birth?" Mr. Stone asked.

Hall said, "At birth I believe his gestational age was thirty-six and six-sevenths weeks, or thirty-seven weeks."

"Let's talk about surfactant," Stone said. "In 1983 when Brett was born, were there any tests for surfactant that could be administered before the baby was born?"

Hall answered, "Not specifically for surfactant, but there are analyses of amniotic fluid that can be performed to check for certain lipids in the fluid."

"How would you get the amniotic fluid?"

Dr. Hall said, "By performing a procedure called amniocentesis."

"What are the reasons for performing the procedure known as amniocentesis?" Stone asked.

Dr. Hall said, "Multiple reasons, mainly two. The first in early second trimester pregnancies to determine the chromosomal complement of the fetus and also to check for certain chemicals that may or may not denote spinal cord problems or brain problems such as spina bifida or anencephaly, and later in the pregnancy they may performed to see if an infant has sufficient quantities of certain lipids that are correlated with mature lungs."

"Well, is that to see if the surfactant is present? Is that what you are telling me?" Stone asked.

Hall said, "I can't make the translation into saying that those tests check for surfactant because I don't think they do, but the correlation of the presence or absence of these lipids exists and the assumption is that there is sufficient surfactant if these lipids exists in certain quantities."

"What are the indications for doing amniocentesis?" Mr. Stone then asked.

"At which point in the pregnancy?" Dr. Hall asked.

"Well, let's talk about the second reason that you gave for doing it to see if these certain lipids are present to gauge the maturity of the lungs," Mr. Stone said. "What are the indications for wanting to do that, for wanting to perform the amniocentesis?"

Dr. Hall replied, "I can only... Well, the main reason is to determine if the baby is mature, and there are many reasons why you would want to do that."

"Was amniocentesis performed at any time during the pregnancy of Brenda Meyer with Brett Meyer?" Mr. Stone asked.

Hall replied, "No, sir."

"Was there ever any indication in your mind for performing amniocentesis during her pregnancy?"

"No, sir."

"You believed Brett Meyer to be mature or a full-term baby, a thirty-seven week baby, when he was born, is that right?"

"Yes, sir."

"Now that was on December twenty-seventh?"

"Yes, sir."

"You had her in the hospital to attempt to induce labor, I think, on December twenty-first, did you not?" Mr. Stone asked.

Hall answered, "The evening of the twenty-first, and the morning and early afternoon of the twenty-second, yes."

Mr. Stone continued, "That was almost a week earlier?"

"Right," Hall responded.

"Did you think about doing amniocentesis on that occasion?" Stone asked.

Dr. Hall said, "I did not."

Stone fired back, "Why not?"

Hall explained, "Because at thirty-six weeks with chronic hypertension and preeclampsia and what I considered to be a deteriorating condition in the mother, I didn't feel it was indicated because if the infant was unable to breathe, it would be very, very rare, and the medical condition of the pregnancy at that point, after having had three and a half weeks of complications, I felt that it warranted delivery."

"Now earlier, I believe around December first or November thirtieth, Brenda Meyer was sent over to the hospital, was she, for some testing on the infant?" Mr. Stone asked.

Dr. Hall replied, "Yes, sir."

"And what was the reason for that?" Stone asked.

Dr. Hall said, "The reason for that was that she reported to me on November thirtieth that she had felt a great deal of movement the day before and none that day, and plus she also had complained of a discharge from the vagina. And I instructed her to come to the office so I would be sure whether or not she had ruptured her membranes at that point, and after that point sent her to the hospital for what we call a non-stress test, and that was mainly because of the complaint of decreased movement at the time."

"Now, if that test had indicated that the fetus was in fact not moving and not responding properly, would you have done a cesarean section at that time?" Mr. Stone asked.

Dr. Hall replied, "The non-stress test? No, sir."

Mr. Stone asked, "What would the next step have been?"

Dr. Hall said, "The next step was that we gave her some time to walk around, we gave her fluids to drink. That sometimes takes a baby and wakes it up out of a sleep cycle, and then we performed another non-stress test, and that was also non-reactive."

"Then what did you do?" Stone asked.

Dr. Hall answered, "Then we did a contraction stress test, or oxytocin challenge test. They are both the same, in my opinion. And we performed that to see if the baby was all right."

"Which test did you actually do?" Stone asked. "Are those two different procedures? You say they are both the same in your opinion. Is that because there is some difference in those procedures but they are basically designed to do the same thing?"

"Someone may have spontaneous contractions," Hall explained. "If they have three contractions within a certain length of time, then that is sufficient criteria for a contraction stress test. It may be spontaneous, it may not. If it is not spontaneous, then we must administer oxytocin or Pitocin to make the contractions happen."

Mr. Stone asked, "How does that drug or chemical make the

contractions happen?"

Hall answered, "Oxytocin or Pitocin is a similar chemical to an endogenous chemical or protein in the body called Pitocin or oxytocin that the pituitary gland makes that makes the uterus contract."

Mr. Stone asked, "What are you looking for when you administer that test?"

Dr. Hall replied, "We are trying to mimic stress or labor, and if the stress or labor are mimicked, if it is produced, then we watch the heart rate of the baby in response to those contractions. And if the baby experiences or exhibits simultaneous repetitive late decelerations of its heart rate in response to the maternal contractions, then it is considered a positive stress test or positive OTC or positive contraction stress test, and that is ominous."

"It's ominous for what?" Stone asked.

"The fetus," Hall responded.

Stone asked, "For what particular condition?"

Hall answered, "It is ominous because it means the uteroplacental blood flow is very compromised and that the placenta, if you will, is ready to wear out."

"And would that mean that the child needs to be delivered?" Mr. Stone asked.

Dr. Hall replied, "At that time, yes, sir."

Stone then asked, "Now, at the time that you did these tests, this was the end of November or the very beginning of December, was it not?"

"It was November thirtieth and December first," Hall responded.

"And what would the gestational age of Brett Meyer have been in your opinion at that time?" Stone asked.

"Thirty-three to thirty-three-and-a-half weeks," Hall answered.

Mr. Stone said, "Now, that would be a significant degree of gestational age prematurity, would it not?"

Dr. Hall replied, "Yes, sir."

"Did you order an amniocentesis to go along with the other tests that you ordered on that occasion?" Mr. Stone asked.

Hall responded, "No, sir."

Stone asked, "Is there a particular reason why you did not?"

"It wasn't indicated," Hall answered.

"What would the indications have been for amniocentesis at that time?" Stone asked.

Hall replied, "With a negative contraction stress test, none."

Mr. Stone asked, "Was there a negative contraction stress test?"

"Yes, sir," responded Dr. Hall.

"Had the contraction stress test been positive, then would you have ordered an amniocentesis?" Stone asked.

Dr. Hall said, "No, sir."

"What would have had to happen in your mind at that particular juncture in time in the beginning of December for you to order an amniocentesis?" Stone asked.

Hall responded, "I can't think of a reason to do one."

Mr. Stone asked, "Would there have been no circumstance, given your own estimate of the child's gestational age, would there have been no reason or circumstance for you to want to know the maturity stage of the child's lungs?"

"I would assume that the lungs would be immature at that point," Hall answered.

"So you would be looking for problems if you had to deliver

the baby at that point, problems with respiration?" Stone asked. "I mean, you would be anticipating that there might be some?"

Dr. Hall replied, "I think there could be some at that point, yes, sir."

"Is amniocentesis to determine the lung maturity of the child basically used in elective situations where the delivery is elective?" Stone continued.

"Not basically, but it may be used in a situation like that," Hall answered.

"When else is it used for that particular purpose, the purpose of determining the maturity of the lungs?" Mr. Stone asked.

Dr. Hall said, "It can be used when there is uncertainty about the patient's gestational age and you are trying to make a decision as to allow the patient to deliver or deliver the patient itself, herself, then it might be helpful to have the status of the lungs of the infant known."

Stone asked, "So, if we can translate that now and apply that description or indication that you just gave to Brenda Meyer's situation, if you had been uncertain as to the gestational age of Brett Meyer on December twenty-seventh before you did the cesarean section, would that have been a time to do amniocentesis to determine the immaturity of his lungs?"

Mr. Brinkman stepped in then. "Let me object to the question. Are you asking him was he certain?"

Mr. Stone answered, "No, if he had been uncertain. I think he's indicated he was certain."

Mr. Brinkman asked, "Are you hypothesizing all the other conditions that existed of the patient? We are talking about this real patient?"

"Well, I didn't, but I think I am." Mr. Stone continued to Dr. Hall, "I'm asking you to consider the situation as it was on December twenty-seventh with the single exception that you are now uncertain about his gestational age. Would that have been an occasion for you to have performed amniocentesis to determine the maturity of the fetus' lungs?"

Mr. Brinkman said, "I would ask one clarification. By 'uncertainty,' within what limitations are you talking about?"

Mr. Stone said, "Well, I think by definition if you are uncertain you are not sure of the limitations."

Mr. Brinkman asked, "Are we eliminating the uncertainties?"

Stone replied, "If you want to qualify your answer by saying there is range of uncertainty that would indicate it, by all means do that. But I'm just asking you if you take the situation as it existed on December 27th, 1983, and the only fact we alter is that, instead of you feeling confident that you knew the gestational age, you would have been uncertain instead. My question is under all those circumstances, would you have requested amniocentesis at that time?"

Dr. Hall said, "I can't answer the question simply. Let me explain why I can't. If I was uncertain of the gestational age, then I would have done an amniocentesis on December twenty-first."

"Now explain to me why you said you would have done it on the twenty-first," Stone requested.

Hall responded, "Well, that is the first time that I made the decision that she needed to be delivered because of her condition."

Mr. Stone then said, "So you are telling me that December twenty-seventh was just like the second act of the play that had begun on December twenty-first, in terms of her condition."

Hall replied, "Actually, the fourth act, but right."

Mr. Stone asked, "You hadn't tried to induce labor in the early part of December. You had started that on the twenty-first, right? Is that what you are referring to?"

Dr. Hall replied, "Yes, the evening of the twenty-first because her condition had deteriorated that day."

"I take it by your answer that what you are saying is when you made the decision to attempt to induce labor that is when you also would have asked for the amniocentesis?" Stone asked.

"If I thought it had been indicated," Hall answered.

Stone asked, "And the reason again that you didn't think it was indicated is that you felt you knew the gestational age of the child?"

"Yes, sir," Hall replied.

Mr. Stone then said, "Now let's move on to the gestational age again, and I'd like you to tell me what are all the ways that you as an obstetrician used in Brenda Meyer's case to judge the gestational age of Brett Meyer as a fetus. I'm going to get down to the particular dates, but I guess what I'm asking you are what various tests, investigations, or whatever you did to tell the gestational age? If you want to give me the dates as you answer, we can do that."

"Many different things are taken into account," Hall replied. "The first is, and often the most reliable, is the first day of the last menstrual period."

Mr. Stone asked, "As related by the mother?"

"As related by the mother and as related by previous records," Dr. Hall answered.

"Did she have any records?" Stone asked.

Hall responded, "Yes, sir."

Mr. Stone asked, "What records did you see?"

Hall said, "The records that I have referred to earlier in our deposition, the first three pages of this chart. Dr. Mason's records were transferred to me when the patient came to see me the first time. So I had those in my possession."

Stone asked, "What did they tell you?"

"They told me two things that were important," Dr. Hall said. "The first is that the first day of her last menstrual period was April

134

11th, 1983, and there wasn't any issue of a question. And the second was a urine pregnancy test had been done on that day, June second, and it was positive."

Stone asked, "What particular significance does that have?"

Dr. Hall said, "Urine pregnancy tests will not turn positive until someone is five to six weeks pregnant or have five to six weeks estimated gestational age or beyond. And hers was positive at six weeks, which is approximately what she was at that point."

"And what other information did you use to assess gestational age?" Mr. Stone asked.

Hall answered, "I also used the initial physical exam that I performed on Brenda in July, July second, and that is also a very sensitive method of determining estimated gestational age."

"And how so?" Stone asked. "What makes it sensitive, and what is the particular procedure that you used to determine gestational age?"

Dr. Hall responded, "A pelvic exam is used, and in trained hands a pregnancy exam in the first trimester is relatively sensitive in estimating gestational age."

Stone asked, "But that is a judgment made by the examiner?"

Hall said, "It is a judgment call made by the examiner, correct."

Mr. Stone asked, "What other means did you use to assess the gestational age?"

Dr. Hall answered, "Sequential physical exams as measuring the fundal height, the fundus of the uterus being the top, and sequential exams using the McDonald system of measurement agreed almost perfectly throughout the whole pregnancy."

"How many of these sequential physical exams did you do?" Stone asked.

"Eleven or twelve," Hall replied.

Stone asked, "And they all agreed with your estimate of gestational age?"

"Yes, sir, they agreed within one centimeter," Hall said. "Do you want me to explain what the McDonald system is?"

"Yes," Stone replied.

Hall said, "The McDonald system of measurement is used after the twentieth week of gestation by measuring from the maternal pubic symphysis in centimeters to the top of the uterine fundus. And the correlation is one centimeter per week of gestation after the twentieth week."

Mr. Stone asked, "What other tests or data did you have to help you judge gestational age?"

"I performed three ultrasound exams," Hall responded.

Stone asked, "What were the dates of the three ultrasounds?"

Hall said, "The first was September third, the second October first, and the last November twelfth."

Stone asked, "What did they show you?"

Dr. Hall answered, "On September third, the ultrasound measurement yielded an estimated gestational age of approximately nineteen weeks by biparietal diameter, and that agreed within ten days of her estimated gestational age by her dates from her last menstrual period."

"Okay," Stone said. "What is biparietal diameter?"

"Biparietal diameter is the measuring between the parietal bones of the fetal skull," Dr. Hall replied.

Mr. Stone asked, "So it's essentially the size of the head?"

"It's one measurement of the size of the head," Hall responded.

"And what did your test on October first tell you, your ultrasound on October first?" Stone asked.

Dr. Hall said, "On October first, the biparietal diameter revealed fifty-four millimeters, which was approximately twenty-two to twenty-three weeks estimated gestational age, and that agreed again within ten days of her estimated gestational age by dates, and it also agreed almost exactly with her previous ultrasound."

"Okay," Mr. Stone said. "What about November twelfth?"

Hall answered, "On November twelfth, that sonogram revealed that the biparietal diameter was seventy-eight to eighty millimeters, and that was consistent with thirty-one weeks estimated gestational age, and that agreed perfectly with her last menstrual period estimated gestational age."

Mr. Stone then asked, "Did these ultrasounds tell you anything else about the fetus other than the biparietal diameter?"

Dr. Hall said, "At that time that's approximately all I was doing, was measuring that, and measuring the fact that amniotic fluid was increased or decreased or adequate and just knowing—also looking at the presentation of the baby, whether it was head first, breach, or transverse."

"Is it a fair statement from your recitation of these tests that you made about gestational age, and particularly the ultrasounds, that you never saw any evidence of intrauterine growth retardation in this infant?" Mr. Stone asked.

Dr. Hall answered, "That's my impression, correct."

"We talked earlier about the oxytocin challenge test and the non-stress test, and you described in some detail the oxytocin challenge test, but I don't think I asked you to tell us how the non-stress test works," Stone then said. "Would you describe that test to us and tell us what it's supposed to do and show?"

"A non-stress test is, has been designed to use an external fetal monitor to record the fetal heart rate, and its purpose is to test for uteroplacental insufficiency," Dr. Hall replied.

Stone asked, "How does it do that?"

"It does it by seeing if the baby's heart rate will increase in response to its own movements," replied Dr. Hall.

Mr. Stone asked, "And is that connected to the sufficiency of the blood supply through the uterus or through the placenta?"

Hall replied, "That is the implication, correct. Plus, it also is a rather rough way of deciding if the infant has an intact neural axis."

"What is the neural axis?" Stone asked.

"In a broad sense just saying if the infant has an intact function of the brain, but that's only in the broadest sense," Dr. Hall answered.

"I take it from your earlier description that the non-stress tests are not conclusive in themselves of anything in particular. They just lead to other detailed examinations," Mr. Stone said.

"That's not quite true," Dr. Hall replied. "I didn't mean to mislead you if I did. The non-stress test, if it is reactive, is highly predictive of an intact uteroplacental blood flow and neural axis. If it is non-reactive, then it suggests that there may not be good things going on."

Stone asked, "When you are through with the non-stress tests and you are sure you have gotten an accurate result, then you move to the oxytocin challenge test, is that correct? If the non-stress tests were non-reactive, you move to the oxytocin challenge test?"

"Yes, sir," Hall answered.

"What I'm saying to you is, now in Brett's case, you had a favorable result from the oxytocin test, is that right?" Mr. Stone asked.

"Yes, sir," Dr. Hall again replied.

Mr. Stone then asked, "What are some of the reasons why he might not have reacted to the non-stress test but did react to the oxytocin test? That's what I meant when I said benign reasons, reasons that the first test might be a non-favorable result and the second one a favorable result."

"I'm not sure I can give you a very good answer," Hall answered. "The simplest thing is to say he was asleep and he finally woke up, but I don't think that's an inclusive list. I'm not an expert in maternal fetal physiology, and I leave those questions usually to the perinatologist."

Stone asked, "What are the ways that the age of a neonate or a newborn infant, the gestational age of a newborn infant, are assessed once the child is born?"

"I really can't answer that," Dr. Hall replied.

Mr. Stone said, "Are you aware that there were several different assessments of Brett Meyer's gestational age at the time of his birth made by the pediatricians who handled him right after he was born, and by the attending nurse, and by the physicians who attended him at Children's Memorial Hospital?"

"Yes," Hall responded.

"And are you aware of the range of those estimates?" Stone asked.

"I am aware that they—I believe I am aware of the range, right," Hall replied.

Mr. Stone said, "And is it fair to say that that range was from thirty-two to thirty-five weeks? I'm sorry, from thirty-two to thirty-seven weeks?"

"That's my understanding," Dr. Hall answered.

Mr. Stone asked, "Are you able to offer any medical explanation for why that range is so large?"

Dr. Hall's only response was, "No, sir."

A brief discussion was held off the record at this point before the deposition continued.

"Perhaps I didn't understand your question," Dr. Hall said.

"Which question are you talking about?" Mr. Stone asked.

"What medical reasons there would be for the range," Hall said. "There were two physicians and one nurse. Of the two physicians, one said thirty-six to thirty-seven weeks, the other one said thirty-five-plus weeks. The nurse said thirty-two weeks based on one measurement of arm recoil. So I can't really speak, I can't answer your question about medical reasons for that, but I can tell you that's my understanding of what the measurements were and how they were arrived at."

"Are you aware that he was labeled premature at Children's Memorial Hospital?" Mr. Stone asked.

Dr. Hall said, "No, I was not aware of that, unless before thirty-seven weeks. If they said he was thirty-five weeks, then it would fit the definition if was before thirty-seven."

Stone asked, "Now, you mentioned that the nurse made a thirty-two week assessment of his gestational age based on one measurement, which was what?"

"Arm recoil is what the chart says," Dr. Hall replied.

Mr. Stone asked, "What does that mean?"

"I don't really know," Hall said.

Mr. Stone then asked, "What is a rollover test?"

Dr. Hall replied, "A rollover test is a test that was devised by some physicians to predict preeclampsia in women who were having their first baby between the twenty-eighth and thirty-second week of pregnancy."

"Is it used only in the first pregnancy? Stone asked.

"That's how it was designed, and that's what its predictive value usually is for," Hall responded.

Stone asked, "Do you use it in the first pregnancy?"

"No, sir," Dr. Hall replied.

Mr. Stone then said, "Now, we've spoken about inducing labor, and I believe we got a little bit into the subject of what that is, but would you now explain to us specifically what the induction of labor is, how it is brought about?"

"The induction of labor is the initiation of the labor process," Dr. Hall replied. "It can be done in different ways."

"Tell me some of those ways," Mr. Stone said.

"Some people feel if you perform amniotomy that that may bring on labor," Hall answered.

Mr. Stone asked, "What is amniotomy?"

"An amniotomy is the artificial rupture of membranes," Dr. Hall responded. "Some people feel that that is one method of inducing labor. Another way to induce labor is to encourage intermittent nipple stimulation to make contractions happen, and sometimes that is an endogenous, if you will, induction. It makes the mother's pituitary glands secrete Pitocin, which makes the uterus contract. Another way to induce labor is to use prostaglandins, which in the last few years have gained some increased use but were not generally available in 1983."

Stone asked, "Is that a hormone?"

"I don't know if it is a hormone," Dr. Hall answered. "It's its own class of chemical category, but there are some prostaglandins which have been recovered from laboring mothers so we know it does make the uterus contract. Another way is to give intravenous Pitocin or oxytocin to the mother to make the uterus contract."

"What were the indications for the induction of labor in Brenda Meyer's case?" Stone asked.

Dr. Hall replied, "The indications for induction of labor were the fact she was thirty-six weeks and had superimposed pre-eclampsia on a chronic hypertensive condition, and she had worsened that day after having been on bed rest for three weeks, was getting worse in that she was having blurred vision. She was having increased blood pressure, and she was starting to spill protein in the urine higher than she had before. And therefore, after her family physician for whom she worked called me and informed me about her blood pressure and informed me about her proteinuria, knowing she was thirty-six weeks, I decided it would be better to deliver her if we could because the only cure for preeclampsia or pregnancy hypertension is delivery."

Mr. Stone asked, "This is on what date that you made this decision?"

"December twenty-first," Dr. Hall replied.

"You had her come into the hospital for that induction, did you not?" Stone then asked.

"Correct," Hall responded.

Stone asked, "And what was her blood pressure in the hospital?"

"Initial blood pressure was 156 over 100," Dr. Hall replied.

"That's when she checked in?" Mr. Stone asked.

Dr. Hall said, "That's at 7:15 p.m., right."

"Now, what other blood pressure readings did you get in the hospital when she was in for induction on the twenty-first?" Stone asked.

"The first reading was 156 over 100," Dr. Hall said. "My first reading after a few minutes was 120 over 100."

Stone asked, "And is that the only reading you got on that hospitalization?"

"No, I took one the next morning, 102 over 70," replied Dr. Hall.

"Would you say that she was in any acute danger from hypertension during that particular period of time that these blood pressure readings were going on?" Mr. Stone asked.

Hall responded, "No, sir."

Mr. Stone then asked, "Now, was a fetal monitor used during that induction?"

"Yes, sir," answered Dr. Hall.

"Did the fetal monitor indicate any fetal distress?" Stone asked.

"Well, I guess it's hard to answer that," Dr. Hall responded. "Could you define for me fetal distress?"

"Well, let me rephrase the question," Mr. Stone said. "Did the fetal monitor indicate to you any reason for intervening beyond the induction process that you were doing?"

"No, sir," Dr. Hall replied.

Stone asked, "Was the reason for that induction process solely that you were concerned about Brenda's hypertension?"

"The reason for the induction process was that she was in a worsening condition," Hall answered.

"As to what?" Mr. Stone asked. "What was worse about her condition?"

Dr. Hall said, "She was spilling protein more than she had before on absolute bed rest, she was seeing spots, she was having headaches, which she hadn't had as much before, and she felt very poorly and the baby had decreased its movements."

"Well, the baby decreased its movements back in the end of November and early December?" Stone said.

"Right," Dr. Hall responded.

"Had you done any further testing to determine whether the baby's movements had been normal in the interim between December first through the twenty-first?" Mr. Stone asked. "What test did you do?"

"Non-stress test," Dr. Hall replied.

Mr. Stone asked, "When was that done?"

"December sixth, thirteenth, and nineteenth," answered Dr. Hall.

Stone asked, "Were those reactive?"

"Yes, sir," said Dr. Hall.

"So the baby was moving then?" Stone asked.

"Right," Hall responded.

Mr. Stone asked, "And you said a reactive non-stress test is conclusive for a healthy condition?"

Dr. Hall responded, "No, sir, I said it is predictive for a supposed intact uteroplacental insufficiency."

"Let me cut to the chase here," Stone said. "Those tests would not have given you a reason to induce labor in themselves, would they?"

"Correct," Dr. Hall said. "The ones on the sixth, thirteenth, nineteenth."

"Now let's talk about proteinuria, or protein in the urine," Mr. Stone then said. "If I remember correctly, you said that Dr. Russell told you she had one-plus on his test in his office?"

"Right," said Dr. Hall.

"And she came to the hospital, and she showed a trace when she checked in?" Mr. Stone asked.

"Right," replied Dr. Hall.

"Were any further urine analyses done for protein?" Stone asked.

"I believe they were done during the induction process," Hall answered.

Mr. Stone asked, "What did they show?"

"I'll have to look through the record, if you don't mind," Hall replied. "At 4:55 a.m. on December twenty-second, albumin was negative," replied Dr. Hall.

Mr. Stone asked, "Albumin is another word for protein?"

"I'm sorry, yes, sir," Hall responded. "It's the same thing. At 7 a.m., albumin negative. At 8:50 a.m., albumin negative. At 1 p.m., trace."

Stone then asked, "So, in terms of protein in the urine, at least while she was in the hospital, the tests that you did in the hospital, can you say that her condition was worsening just with regard to that one item?"

"I can't answer yet," Dr. Hall answered. "Let me finish, please. The last one was negative. That was at 4:30 p.m. No, it wasn't worsening at that point."

"Was she still reporting spots before her eyes while she was still in the hospital?" Mr. Stone asked.

"No, sir," Dr. Hall replied.

"Was she still reporting headaches?"

"No, sir."

"You have used the word 'preeclampsia' several times to describe, I guess, a condition." Mr. Stone then said. "A medical condition. Would you tell us what that is?"

Dr. Hall said, "Preeclampsia is a disorder of maternal blood pressure that occurs usually in primigravida, which is first-pregnancy women, but can occur in other pregnancies and frequently occurs with people with chronic hypertension in subsequent pregnancies, and is loosely defined as an elevation in blood pressure of thirty systolic or fifteen diastolic over baseline, with increase in urine protein. And one of the old definitions used to include edema, but that's not very important anymore."

Mr. Stone then asked, "Now, in terms of Brenda's hospital stay, while you were trying to induce labor, did she demonstrate an

145

elevation of thirty millimeters of mercury over her systolic base-line?"

"On one occasion she did on emission, and on one occasion she did an hour later," Hall answered.

Mr. Stone then asked, "How about a fifteen millimeter increase in diastolic? Did she demonstrate that during the hospital stay when you were attempting induction of labor on the twenty-first or twenty-second?"

Dr. Hall answered, "Yes, sir, she did."

Stone asked, "On how many occasions?"

"One occasion by me, four occasions by the nurses," Dr. Hall responded.

"Out of... You read about a dozen or so measurements?" Stone asked.

"I think I read more than a dozen, twenty or thirty," Dr. Hall said.

"The bottom line is she went home on the twenty-second, and you didn't deem it necessary at that point to do a cesarean section or do any other intervention?" Mr. Stone pointed out. "You thought it was reasonable to allow her to go home for the holidays?"

"Well, I had trouble with that decision, but I did let her go," Dr. Hall answered.

"Was she in any acute distress when you let her go or at any acute risk?" Mr. Stone asked. "I should rephrase that. Was there any serious risk in letting her go home?"

"No, sir, not serious risk," Hall replied.

Stone then asked, "When she went home on the twenty-second, it was prearranged she would come back in on the twenty-seventh, five days later?"

"No, sir. Actually, it had been arranged before that," Dr. Hall replied.

"When was it arranged?" Stone asked.

Dr. Hall said, "I believe it was arranged on the nineteenth that she was going to come in on the twenty-seventh for induction of labor."

Mr. Stone said, "So you had, aside from any emergency situation that you thought she was having on the twenty-first, you had already on the nineteenth decided to try to induce labor on the twenty-seventh?"

"At thirty-seven weeks, correct," Hall said.

Stone asked, "Why?"

"Because she had pregnancy-induced hypertension with chronic hypertension, and she had been on bed rest for three weeks and wasn't going to get any better until we delivered the baby, and that's when I thought it would be safe to deliver," Dr. Hall responded.

Mr. Stone asked, "So you were going to deliver this baby on the twenty-seventh if you could?"

"Yes, sir," Dr. Hall answered.

"On the nineteenth, were you contemplating to do a cesarean section on the twenty-seventh?" Stone asked.

"No, sir," Dr. Hall responded.

Mr. Stone asked, "And if she had come in on the twenty-seventh, without this intervening episode on the twenty-first, just according to your plan on the nineteenth and you had been unable to induce labor, as it turned out you were on the twenty-seventh, would you have then done a cesarean section?"

"I don't know," Hall responded.

"Now let's move on to the twenty-seventh," Stone continued. "She comes back to the hospital. An induction of labor is attempted again, is that right?"

"Right," Hall replied.

Stone asked, "What was her blood pressure when she got back to the hospital on the twenty-seventh?"

"100 over 50 is the emission blood pressure," Hall answered. "Yes, that's right, 100 over 50."

Stone asked, "And that's normal, isn't it?"

"Yes, sir," Hall answered.

"And read to us the blood pressures that were taken during the attempted induction on the twenty-seventh, prior to the cesarean section." Mr. Stone directed.

"The first one you have," Dr. Hall responded. "The next one is 130 over 80, 128 over 82, 110 over 60, 110 over 70, 112 over 70, 110 over 70, 130 over 80, 136 over 86, 112 over...I think it's 88."

Mr. Stone asked, "Now, those are all within normal range, aren't they?"

"All but one, I guess," Hall answered. "The eighty-six is a little high. The eighty-eight is a little high on the diastolic, but it's borderline. The rest were pretty normal."

"In terms of her blood pressure, was there any acute emergency or any serious emergency going on during that period of time that those readings were taken?" Mr. Stone asked.

"I'm not sure I understand what you are saying by acute emergency," Hall replied.

Stone asked, "Was there any emergency need to do a cesarean section because of her blood pressure on that date?"

"At that minute, no, not an emergency," Dr. Hall answered.

"Now let's talk about protein in the urine or albumin in the urine," Stone then said. "What tests were done during the hospitalizations of December twenty-seventh to determine that factor?"

"Let me refer to the lab first," Dr. Hall said. "Upon admission, she had a trace of protein, December twenty-seventh. And I'll go through the labor record here and see what else she had. 'A.M., albumin negative; 11:22 a.m., albumin negative; 2 p.m., complaint of headache.' That's it."

Mr. Stone then asked, "So, in terms of albumin or protein in the urine, there was no alarming finding during that hospitalization, was there?"

Hall responded, "Not that day, no, sir."

"And she complained of a headache on one occasion you read?" Mr. Stone asked.

"One occasion, but I think she says it's from not eating or something like that," Dr. Hall answered.

Stone asked, "No serious headaches?"

"No."

"No spots before the eyes?"

"None complained of," Dr. Hall answered.

"Now, was the fetal monitor tape used, or fetal monitor used to measure the heart rate of that infant?" Mr. Stone then asked.

"Yes, sir," Dr. Hall said.

Mr. Stone asked, "And did that indicate that there was any medical reason, in terms of the condition of the infant, to perform a cesarean section?"

"Based on the heart rate tracing that day?" Dr. Hall asked.

"Based on anything you found that day," Stone asked. "I'm specifically asking about the fetal monitoring."

"Based on the fetal heart rate tracing, the fetal monitoring, no, no sign of bradycardia or late decelerations," Dr. Hall replied.

Mr. Stone asked, "Were there any other tests that indicated, based on the condition of the infant, that he should be delivered that day?"

"Just the whole month before," Hall responded.

"You are referring to…" Stone asked.

Hall answered, "The whole gestalt of everything put together is what led to the decision to go ahead with the delivery because the inductions had failed twice, spread a week apart in a multiparous lady, so the decision was made to deliver the baby."

"Based upon the lab tests and the blood pressure readings and the nurse's observations of Brenda Meyer on the twenty-seventh, was there any danger in allowing the pregnancy to continue as of that date?" Mr. Stone then asked.

"Yes, sir," answered Dr. Hall.

Stone asked, "What was that danger?"

"The danger is placental abruption," fired back Dr. Hall. "The danger is a maternal stroke, seizures, still birth."

"When did those particular dangers become factors in your thinking with Brenda Meyer?" Mr. Stone quickly asked.

"July second," Hall responded.

"So those dangers hadn't changed?" Stone asked.

"No, sir," Dr. Hall replied.

"The only difference was that now you thought the baby was full term and could be delivered electively?" Stone clarified.

"No, that's not the only difference," Dr. Hall replied. "The other difference was that she had had an exacerbation of her symptoms and signs despite absolute bed rest."

Mr. Stone asked, "But she wasn't having those exacerbations on the twenty-seventh?"

"Correct," Hall answered.

Mr. Stone then said, "I guess my question is, on the twenty-seventh, was there anything about her condition that indicated any greater risk of these four adverse results—abruption of the placenta, maternal stroke, seizures, or stillbirth—was there any greater risk of those on the twenty-seventh than there had been on July second?"

"Absolutely," Hall responded.

"And what made you feel that there was a greater risk on the twenty-seventh?" Stone asked.

"The longer a pregnancy goes when someone has chronic hypertension, the more likely those bad things are to happen," Dr. Hall answered.

"We've talked about your reasons for wanting to induce labor," Stone said. "Now I want to go specifically to the decision to do the cesarean section. Will you tell me all the reasons you had for deciding on the evening of the twenty-seventh of December to perform a cesarean section on Brenda Meyer?"

"I can," Dr. Hall replied. "I performed a cesarean section at that time because it was my belief that delivery was indicated. Conventional methods of getting her to deliver were not successful in three different attempts, the evening of the twenty-first, the day of the twenty-second, and all the day of the twenty-seventh. For whatever reason, her cervix was not opening, and I was unable to give her more Pitocin to make it open anymore.

"This is an individual that I had been worried about for six months, or five and a half months," Hall continued, "and feeling very certain from the methods that I had that the baby should be mature and that she had chronic hypertension, she had a failed induction. My belief was that the delivery was indicated and a cesarean section was a logical consequence as a method of delivery.

151

"Also, I remember very specifically having a discussion with Brenda and Keith and their raising their concern that they wanted the baby delivered and basically that they requested it, not that that would have changed my mind or that would have given me the idea. I don't mean it that way, but they were clearly aware that I felt delivery was necessary and it wasn't a flippant, quick decision. It was a decision made with five and a half months of evidence and the previous four weeks of real worry, including having the patient contact me over Christmas every day to see how she was doing.

"So I did a C-section because it was the best way to get the baby delivered. Whether it was vaginal or C-section, it's not important. Delivery was to be done, and that's why I did it," finished Hall

"Now, I have a couple of questions about things that you may have said to the Meyers after the baby was born," Mr. Stone said. "The first thing is did you ever offer to allow Keith Meyer to stay with you so he didn't have to commute back and forth to the hospital?"

"I don't remember," replied Dr. Hall.

"Is it possible that you did?" Stone asked.

"It's possible," responded Hall.

Mr. Stone then asked, "Did you at any time offer to loan money to Brenda Meyer?"

"I don't recall that I did," replied Hall.

"Is it possible that you did?" Stone asked.

"I don't think so," Hall responded.

"Brenda Meyer alleges that, in retrospect, she remembers you saying on several occasions after the baby was born that you were sorry," Stone then said. "Do you remember saying that you were sorry?"

"I may have," Dr. Hall answered.

"Now, did you ever ask her to write a letter on your behalf, telling her that your actions in her case were being reviewed by your hospital?" Stone asked.

Hall responded, "Yes, I did."

"And were your actions reviewed?" Stone asked.

"They were," Dr. Hall answered.

Mr. Stone asked, "And were you subjected to any censure or discipline?"

"No," Hall answered.

"Were your actions approved by the hospital?" Stone asked.

Dr. Hall said, "Yes, sir."

Mr. Stone continued with several more questions about where the doctor attended medical school, where he received his training in obstetrics and gynecology. After reading through the doctor's deposition, I was amazed how confident he was regarding his care during Brenda's pregnancy and the circumstances revolving around how he eventually delivered the baby.

I was also surprised to read that Dr. Hall started his practice on July 1, 1983. Brenda's first appointment with the doctor was the next day, July second. I found his answer about Brett's gestational age when he was born very interesting. How would a jury digest all the different facts in this case?

CHAPTER 11

Brett was ten years old and growing like a weed. His increasing size and weight were starting to become a problem, especially for Brenda. Getting Brett dressed in the mornings was difficult for Brenda because his bed was so low to the floor. Bending for long periods of time put a strain on her back. Bathing Brett was the hardest because his body was getting so long. Lifting him in and out of the tub became my job because Brenda couldn't do it anymore. It was hard for me to do also, especially when he was wet. I was really concerned for his safety whenever it came time to lift his slippery body up and out of the tub.

Most of his time in the house was spent on the floor. He could crawl from his room to the living room in a flash. His method of crawling was not the usual hands and knees, but dragging himself by his arms and elbow while kicking his strait legs through the entire house. Sometimes if he was in an open area, he would just go into a roll to get where he wanted. Because Brett was on the floor the majority of the time, we put his TV, radio/cassette player, and other things where he could easily access them on the floor. Just like any other kid, he played his video games and listened to his music. He loved to record songs off the radio and play them back, over and over again. He also would spend hours and hours listening to the Cardinals, the Blues, and the Missouri football and basketball teams. One time a close friend asked Cardinal broadcaster Jack Buck to say hi to Brett on the radio during a ball game. I will never forget Brett's face when Jack mentioned Brett's name during the game. It was priceless!

One night as I was getting Brett ready for a bath, I became very angry after making a very disturbing discovery. When I took off Brett's shirt, I found several bruises on his back. They were mainly on his left side and started just below his neck, going down to his belt line. Some of them were at least four or five inches long.

After I called Brenda to come into his room, we both asked him how he got the bruises. He told us it happened at school and it wasn't his fault. He wouldn't tell us what happened, though. He just kept saying it wasn't his fault.

154

As bad as it looked, it didn't seem like he was in any discomfort. I couldn't figure out what would have made such marks on his back. After I gave him a bath, I put him in bed and took some pictures of the damage on his body. I asked him again how it happened, but he never gave me an answer.

Brenda and I tried to figure out how to handle this situation. We didn't want to go to the school making accusations, at least not yet. Our confidence in how the school would investigate was lacking just a bit. I told Brenda to write a note to the teacher and ask if anything unusual happened at school to cause the marks on his back.

The next day when Brett arrived home on the bus, we found a very interesting note from the teacher. The teacher said she had also questioned the same marks on his back after she lifted up his shirt the day before. Why was the teacher lifting up our son's shirt at school! There was no reason for her to be doing so. Brenda and I were really pissed.

This was the third time Brett had come home from school with visible marks on his body. The first was the day I picked him up at afterschool care with the big gash on his forehead that probably should have had stitches. The second was just over a month earlier than the last incident. Brett came home with some funny marks on his throat. Those marks were also long and dark in color.

Brenda and I took off work the next day and went to the Department of Family Services. We filed a complaint of abuse against the teacher. Family Services did do a thorough investigation, but in the end there was not enough proof to proceed any further.

Our legal case still had four depositions that needed to be done. Both sides were going to have two experts giving testimony regarding their views of what actually caused Brett's cerebral palsy. Doctor Hall's legal team would have an obstetrics and gynecology specialist with a subspecialty in fetal medicine. This person also had expertise in high-risk pregnancies, especially those involving preeclampsia, high blood pressure, and maternal high blood pressure. The defendant's other expert would have a specialty in pediatric neurology.

Our experts also specialized in obstetrics and pediatric neurology. After each deposition was taken, a copy of the proceedings would come in the mail a few days later. After reading each deposition over and over, I wondered how a jury would react to their testimony. Out of the four depositions, one of them really stood out in my mind. This person was our expert in pediatric neurology. Dr. Thompson helped get the lawsuit started with his opinions regarding the cause of Brett's cerebral palsy. He was a well-seasoned expert and, for what he was costing us, should be producing results.

On February seventh, our attorney and the defendant's insurance attorney, Mr. Wilson, both traveled to Chicago, Illinois, for the deposition of our expert witness, Dr. Thompson. He was in Chicago testifying in court regarding another pediatric neurology medical case. He agreed to do the deposition as long as he was allowed to catch his return flight to New York late that afternoon. Mr. Wilson started off questioning Dr. Thompson about his experience and qualifications as an expert in pediatric neurology, all of which were outstanding.

He then asked Dr. Thompson, "Could you briefly give me an overview of the opinions that you've formulated in this case, and we'll go back and try to discuss them more specifically."

Here was the doctor's brief answer:

"They belong to three different categories. The first is what is wrong with this boy, and I believe that his diagnosis is one of cerebral palsy, spastic diplegia. It's a form of having all four limbs involved, with relative sparing about the head and neck, and therefore basically preservation of verbal intelligence, preservation of reasonably good diction or articulation, freedom from seizures, and, I don't know if I mentioned it, normal cephaly, the absence of microcephaly.

"And I think that is basically his diagnosis. He has learning difficulties, despite what I think may be fairly good verbal intelligence. By the mother's account, he was performing not much more than first grade level when he was ten years old. So whatever his IQ is, he wasn't translating it into much academic success at that point.

"And I think he will not have seizures in the future. I think he does have orthopedic problems, and he's had surgery for them. As you know, he's had hamstring releases, and heel-cord releases, and hip-abductor releases. So I think his vision is adequate. His hearing is adequate, and I think he is a healthy boy in general.

"So that's his diagnosis. As relates his prognosis, I think it is possible, but unlikely, that he will walk functionally independently. I think he will be able to manage some of his self-help needs. He is able to feed himself with simple utensils, albeit using a special spoon. He can help in dressing himself, and I think he can manage somehow to get on and attend to some of his toilet functions. But I think in the future he will need some help, at least in part, for things certainly like laces, snaps, zippers, buttons, grooming activities, shampooing his hair, shaving. So he'll never be competent to care for all of his personal needs with his hands. I think there will be academic progress, but he will remain quite a bit behind.

"I was asked specifically by Mr. Stone to comment what his life expectancy may be, and his should be essentially normal. There are reasons for children with CP to have truncated life expectancies, and many do. But none of the factors that generate that reduction are present here.

"Secondly, I don't think he'll be commercially employable. His intellect might be one that would enable him to use his abilities, but if he's started off as suboptimally academically as he has, I don't think he will get enough skill to support himself by his education. And since he has limited locomotion and hand usage, I think, more likely than not, he will not be employable.

"That's about the end of my prognosis. The third part, third question, is what caused his difficulty, and I think to go into the cause you start first with the anatomic basis for his disability, which is damage to the white matter of the brain in the subependymal area, which goes by the acronym PVL.

"The PVL, I think, came because of the combination of his having an immature germinal matrix and superimposed hypoxia reflected by the respiratory difficulty he had after birth, which difficulty, obviously, led to his being transferred to Children's Memorial

Hospital appropriately for tertiary care and which, more likely than not, was associated with some degree of persistent fetal circulation and persistent pulmonary hypertension.

"That's really all I have to say, you know, in terms of broad strokes. I'm not going—I will not be commenting on—I've not been asked to give any opinion about the standard of care. I'll leave that up to other experts to comment on. I will not be expressing any opinions. I think to suggest I have no opinions may not be... I haven't been asked to express any, and I do not plan to offer any."

I think Dr. Thompson's brief answer took the defendant's attorney by surprise. The doctor's answer was very direct, to the point, and probably covered the attorney's first twenty questions. I was glad this guy was on our side. Dr. Thompson answered several more questions regarding Brett's current condition and why different parts of his body were more involved concerning the cerebral palsy.

The expert doctor was then asked, "Do you have any opinions regarding the future care that Brett will require?"

"I don't think Brett's ever going to live by himself. His care is divided into the following categories: He does need and should benefit from therapy, PT and OT. I don't think he needs speech therapy. Hopefully some of these are provided at school, but school is only 182 days per year. So he should have PT probably twice and OT probably twice per week, and I think he should have that until eighteen or twenty-one and then half that thereafter, once a week.

"He will need supervision by physicians. I don't think he will have any more surgery, but he should have an orthopedist or a neurologist follow him. They have to give the prescriptions to the therapist.

"He will need a wheelchair. And when he's older, it may be appropriate to get him a motorized wheelchair. It will give him much more freedom.

"He may need some AFO's, braces around his ankles to make sure he doesn't have a recurrence of what led to the first lengthening of his heel cords. Then, of course, he is going to need—I think he will make judgments for himself, but he will need someone to help him physically. I can't envision him telling his mother at the age of twenty that he's going to go live by himself and take his own apartment, you know. So I think he will need an aide or somebody to help him.

"That's basically the outline, in my opinion."

Mr. Wilson then asked, "What is your opinion as to Brett's gestational age at the time of delivery?"

"I'll yield to an obstetrician," Dr. Thompson replied. "The record gives dates that range from as little as thirty-two weeks to as much as thirty-five weeks. I think he was under thirty-six weeks in any event, but I will yield to an obstetrician."

Wilson asked, "You indicated that Brett suffered from hypoxia after birth?"

"Yes," responded the expert.

"What was the cause of that hypoxia?" Mr. Wilson asked.

"I think hyaline membrane disease or respiratory distress syndrome," Dr. Thompson responded. "I use these terms interchangeably—immature lungs."

Mr. Wilson asked, "Is that the only cause of his respiratory difficulties?"

"I think so," Thompson replied.

"Are there any other possible causes?" Wilson asked.

Dr. Thompson answered, "Well, if he had persistent fetal circulation, and there's a question as to whether he did or didn't, but I won't argue whether he did or didn't, that would have come from hypoxia, and that would have compounded it."

"How was he treated initially, first at St. Joe's and then subsequently at Children's Memorial Hospital, regarding his respiratory distress problems?" Mr. Wilson then asked.

"Given oxygen," Dr. Thompson replied.

Mr. Wilson asked, "Was he on a ventilator?"

"I think he was, yes," answered Dr. Thompson.

"What is the purpose of putting a patient in Brett's condition on a ventilator?" Wilson asked.

"I think to compensate for their immature lungs, for their RDS," Dr. Thompson replied. "I think if persistent fetal circulation hurts, it hurts because you are not getting adequate oxygenation, and then the ventilator would help. The use of the ventilator is helpful, but it also contributes to PVL. It is a factor to help contribute to PVL. This boy had—many children born given his weight breathe fine, and they don't need oxygen, and they don't need to stay in the hospital more than a couple of days, and they don't develop hyaline membrane disease or persistent fetal circulation. They go home. He didn't. He obviously didn't have well-developed lungs, which set into chain a whole group of events, which I think contributed to his developing PVL."

Wilson asked, "How does the ventilator contribute to the PVL?"

"It's the fluctuating pressure," the doctor responded. "Ventilators—it's not only hypoxia, its hypoperfusion, increased venous pressure, fluctuating blood pressure, a whole bunch of factors will damage the germinal matrix. The kid on the ventilator is also on the ventilator because he is not breathing well. But there is a correlation between ventilators and damage to the PVL. I am not sure what came first."

Mr. Wilson asked, "You can't say in this case whether the damage occurred before the ventilator or after the ventilator?"

"That's correct," the doctor responded.

"The ventilator is what necessitated to his RDS? Wilson asked.

"Yes," Thompson answered.

Mr. Wilson then asked, "If you assume that Brett was at thirty-seven weeks in gestation, what percentage of children born at that level of gestation have immature lungs?"

"Small percentage," the doctor responded.

"Can you quantify that?" Wilson asked.

"I don't know. I don't know," Dr. Thompson said. "They are not immune from having it. But obviously it's a much smaller number than those born at thirty-one weeks."

Wilson then asked, "In addition to hypoxia after birth as being a cause of some of Brett's difficulties, you've also indicated that he had an immature germinal matrix. What is that?"

The expert witness said, "That's... I think the essence of it, if you are immature and you are not fully cooked when you are born, there are two things that set you up for CP. One is the germinal matrix, which is the gelatinous area of very, very fragile capillaries around the ventricles, which will bleed if insulted or will soften if insulted to increasing degrees the further away you are from being mature to term. If he had a fully developed germinal matrix which he had...it disappears at birth basically. If his had been fully matured and disappeared, then he could have all the hypoxia he had and not be damaged. If he had the same germinal matrix and didn't have RDS, he probably would have ended up all right.

"He needed two things. He needed to have blood vessels that were vulnerable and a respiratory system which was vulnerable. And it was his luck at the time of birth, even though he was relatively big for children getting into this kind of trouble—I mean this kind of trouble is the rule when you are under thirty-two weeks of gestation. Fifty percent of babies will be bleeding into their brain, but this child ended up with a combination of both, which I think in the end is responsible for his present disability."

"As I understand it, is what you are saying is that it was a combination of his RDS plus his immature germinal matrix that resulted in his current condition?" Mr. Wilson asked.

"Yes," the doctor said. "I believe if he had stayed where he was for another two weeks—I'm not opining whether this was good medical care or not—he would have had...his germinal matrix would have been all resolved, and his lungs would be fully developed, and he wouldn't have this problem."

Mr. Wilson asked, "What do you mean where he was, in the womb? In utero?"

"Yes," he responded. "That's the essence of what I'm saying. So, it's two—there are two vulnerabilities that he had to embrace, or two risks. When he came out early, his brain was vulnerable by having fragile vessels, and his lungs were vulnerable by not being well developed. And the combination of two of these... The amount of oxygen deprivation would not have hurt a seven-and-a-half pound baby, and the amount of immaturity of his brain blood vessels would not have hurt him if he turned out to breathe well and was oxygenated well. So it really is two parts that have to come together to produce this. And I concede that these are not nearly as common when you weigh over 2,000 grams as they are when you weigh under 1,500 grams."

Wilson then asked, "By his size, he was—if he's thirty-one weeks or thirty-two weeks, as you've stepped back, and go to the limit of prematurity or level of maturity, he would be an extremely large baby for thirty-two weeks gestation, wouldn't he?"

"Yes, that's true," Dr. Thompson said.

"Is his weight at delivery more consistent with thirty-seven weeks gestation?" Wilson asked.

"No, I don't think thirty-seven weeks," the doctor answered. "At thirty-six weeks, he weighed 2,500 grams. He is under that. His weight was probably average for thirty-five weeks. But the problem is this: Not everybody is the same. I am not going to be opining about this, but there are means of ascertaining whether the lungs are mature or not, and that issue is whether one should make a guess. But now we're walking into the area of standard of care, and I'm not planning to talk about that."

Mr. Wilson asked, "With regard to the injury that Brett has, are there any events that can occur in utero which would account

162

for the injury to the PVL, or the PVL as you've described it?"

"No, I don't think, not in this case," Dr. Thompson replied. "He came out in good shape. His Apgars were good. His pH was fine. Then he developed breathing difficulties. I think it's clearly—I mean, the classic cause of CP in a vulnerable child is breathing difficulty after birth, and he had it. Again, I believe he was not injured before birth. I believe that if he had stayed in utero for another two weeks, he would be fine, possibly a week. I don't know. I mean, certainly until his lungs were mature, he'd be fine."

After reading through the last few pages of this expert's deposition, something strange hit me. I read the pages and testimony again. Right in front of me in black and white was the answer to the question that we had been looking to find for such a long time. It was the cause of Brett's disability. We now knew what injured his brain. Whether it was the doctor's fault or not, I finally had the closure we had been looking for to put this behind us. There was no more reason in my mind to continue blaming ourselves for Brett's condition. What was done was done, and there was nothing anyone could do to change it. This case was over in my opinion. A jury would ultimately have to make the decision of who was right or wrong. Win, lose, or draw, I needed to stop looking backwards and start thinking about the future ahead. I knew both good and bad days were ahead. It was time to quit worrying about the past.

CHAPTER 12

The days and months started passing very quickly. With all the depositions finalized, plans were being made to move on to trial. Preliminary plans were for the trail to begin early the next year. Mr. Stone was in constant contact with the defendant's attorney, negotiating for an out of court settlement.

I had been preparing for a showdown with the school district for several months. Our main concern was all the children Brett's age were moving on to middle school. The middle school in our district did not provide services for special needs children. The school district planned on leaving Brett at the elementary school until he was high school age.

This was totally unacceptable! Brett needed to be with children his own age. For several months, I visited other school districts to see what services they were required to offer special needs children and was amazed by what they were providing. All the other schools found ways of integrating the disabled kids with the normal kids. This was exactly what we were looking for.

I had more homework to do before approaching the school district, though. I talked to different advocacy agencies regarding accessibility issues and other problems. I made several calls to the state board of education about the issues we had with our school district. They were very helpful and instructed me on how I should proceed with our grievances. It was all a great learning experience.

Once I had all my ducks in a row, I made an appointment with the assistant superintendent of the school district. We met one afternoon just after the school year ended. I told him all the issues we had regarding the education of our son. After I finished, he told me he understood our concerns, but there was nothing the district could do to change the services they provided at that time.

I held my composure the best I could and then told him that if the district could not provide the services we required, then by law they needed to contract with a school district that could. The assistant superintendent kind of smiled and told me he didn't think that was really possible.

Again, I did my best to hold my composure and told him the district would be receiving a registered letter very soon informing them we were filing due process regarding our grievances. I also informed him that we were filing a complaint with the state board of education demanding an investigation of why our school district was not required to provide these services by law.

The school district had ten days to respond to our letter once we filed due process. The district did respond, requesting we schedule a meeting to discuss our differences. We asked that the meeting be scheduled soon because we wanted as much time as possible to finish our dispute before the new school year.

Brenda and I didn't know what to expect when we arrived at the meeting to discuss our problems with the district. There were several rumors going around town that we were suing the school district. Small towns are bad about that, and we were on top of the list for gossip.

Brenda and I were very surprised by what the school district was proposing for Brett's further education. Their plan was to move Brett from the elementary school straight to the high school. At first we didn't like the idea, but when we listened to how they planned on having him interact with all the older kids, it started to grab our interest. We also knew Gina would be able to see what was going on. Plus, all of her friends absolutely loved him. We eventually gave in to the district's proposal, but we would be watching very closely to how he responded to his new surroundings.

Brett did thrive in his new setting. He loved being around the older kids, and he started to mature before our eyes. Gina and her friends made his transition to a new environment a great experience.

As the holidays quickly approached, we received notice from our attorney that our trial was scheduled to begin on March twentieth of next year. Five days were being allotted for the trial. After eight long years we were finally starting to see the light at the end of the tunnel.

My attention quickly started to focus on my brother. He was rapidly losing his fight with cancer. The doctors told him that the treatments were no longer helping. The cancer had spread throughout his entire body. The only thing they could do at that point was keep him as comfortable as possible.

He was having good days, and then he would get very sick and have to go to the hospital. The doctors would pump him full of steroids and other drugs, and then he would get better. These cycles got worse as time went by. I started spending nights with him while he was in the hospital. I would come home after work and spend time with Brenda and kids, and after dinner I would head back to the hospital and spend the night with him. I usually left for work the next morning around 6 a.m. The doctors told me my brother had three to six months left at the most. I made a promise to myself not to let him die alone.

One night as we watched the late evening news, I asked my brother some very tough questions. I said, "Gary, do you have most of your affairs in order?"

He looked at me and said, "I'm not ready to talk about that yet."

"At some point we need to have that conversation, though," I said.

"I signed a form yesterday. I don't want any measures taken to bring me back if something happens."

I sat there a second and then said, "That's your decision." After another moment, I said, "Gary, is there anything special you want to do with the time you have left? Is there a place you want to go or anything else?"

He sat there a second and said, "I would like to go to a hockey game."

"Get yourself well enough to come home from the hospital, and I'll take care of the rest."

At work the following morning, I talked to my boss and

asked him if he could help me out. I told him about my brother's request for some tickets to a hockey game. I knew some of our subcontractors had season tickets to different events and gave them to their employees and other companies. My boss had worked with Gary for several years and told me he would see what he could do.

The next day, he called me into his office. He told me he called our company's corporate headquarters and talked to the vice president of the company. He then handed me a large envelope containing twenty-five tickets to our company's corporate suite for an approaching hockey game. I was overwhelmed by the gift they were giving my brother. I was so proud to work for such great people. When I told Gary what the company was doing for him, he broke down in tears.

The thought of going to the hockey game in a few weeks brightened my brother's spirits. He was even well enough to come home later that week. He had two weeks to think about who he was going to invite to the game.

One evening while I was cooking supper, the phone rang. It was Mr. Stone. He informed us that a settlement offer had been received from Dr. Hall's legal representation. Even though the settlement offer was very low, it still needed to be considered. The offer was substantial enough to pay off our increasing balance with our attorney and still leave enough money to buy some of the medical equipment we needed so much. I asked Mr. Stone his thoughts about the offer on the table. He quickly told me that this was just a game that the other side would play as we approached our trial date. He promised me more substantial offers were possible as time passed.

A few weeks later, another call came from our attorney. This one was much different than all the others we had received over the years. Mr. Stone told us he had great news. He had received another settlement offer. This one was much better than the previous offer, one we might consider taking. The suspense was killing me. "How serious is the offer?" I finally asked.

Mr. Stone said, "It's a very substantial offer. Eight hundred and fifty thousand dollars."

I looked across the room at Brenda. She looked back at me and said, "What?"

I put my hand over the receiver and said, "Eight hundred and fifty thousand dollars!" Brenda's jaw almost hit the floor.

"What do you think, Norm?" I asked. "What do you suggest?"

"The answer will ultimately have to come from you and Brenda," Mr. Stone said. "I will advise you, though, this is a good offer, and probably the last one we will receive before we go to trial in less than three weeks. You and Brenda need to give this great thought. If you do decide to reject this offer, we will without a doubt move on to trial, where a jury will make the final decision. Whatever your decision is, I can promise that I will give you the best legal representation possible until the conclusion of this case. Please contact me as soon as possible with your decision."

Brenda and I talked for hours about the decision we needed to make. Brenda mentioned that eight hundred and fifty thousand dollars was a lot of money and it could buy the necessary equipment we needed at this point and in the future. I agreed that it was an enormous amount of money, but in the end Brett would probably only end up with around four hundred and seventy-five thousand dollars after paying off the account balance with the law firm. Plus, there was the forty percent they were entitled to if the case moved to trial.

It was a very tough decision to make, but in the end we concluded that if the money was invested and handled correctly, it could take care of Brett's needs for a long, long time. We accepted the offer.

Accepting the offer started a whole new process that we would have to go through before the money could be turned over to Brett. Mr. Stone advised us that we needed to find another attorney at that point to represent Brett. He suggested we find a lawyer closer to home that would be more familiar with the circuit court in our county.

Because Brett was still a minor, Brenda and I needed to petition the court to be appointed conservators over his soon-to-be-formed estate. Once Brett received his settlement, a circuit court judge would have to approve how the money was invested or how the money could be spent on Brett's behalf. The whole process would take several weeks.

A couple weeks later, my brother took a turn for the worse. It was apparent that his time was drawing near. At that point I was spending all the time I could with him, only leaving him to go to work. I came home one Saturday morning to put my paycheck in the bank and get some clean clothes, and Brenda asked me to stay home and rest. She wanted me to go to a wedding and reception for some close friends of ours later that day. She understood when I told her I needed to be with my brother.

Late that evening, Gary and I had watched a ball game on his room TV. I remember looking over at him and noticing he had drifted off to sleep. The nurse came in around 11 p.m. with some meds and to do his vitals. When she went to wake him up, he didn't move. She immediately checked to see if he was breathing. He was. She called for a doctor, and I asked the nurse if I should call in the rest of the family. She told me it was time.

It was after midnight. Brenda said she had just gotten home from the wedding reception when I called. She told me she would call my mom and they would be down as soon as possible. Gina had just gotten home from a date, so she would be with Brett.

I will never forget that night and early morning. The doctor wanted a test done to check for brain activity. The nurse said they were very short on staff that night and she was going to have to take him downstairs herself for the test. I asked if I could go along and help. She accepted. We took the elevator down to one of the lowest levels underneath the hospital. I figured out quickly that the nurse was lost. It seemed like we were going in circles, running into doors that would not open and banging into walls. My brother still lay motionless.

When we finally got back to his room, it was 2:30 a.m. and he was still unconscious. About fifteen minutes later, my mom and

Brenda walked into the room. I told them what had been going on. My mother walked around the bed to his side and grabbed his hand in tears. She started talking to his motionless body.

Suddenly his eyes opened, and he said, "What?"

I stood in amazement as he started talking to my mother. Was I going crazy? The nurse and I had spent hours trying to wake him up, banging into doors and walls, and then my mother touches his hand and he wakes up.

By that time I was physically and mentally drained. My mother told me to go home with Brenda and get some rest. She told me she would stay with Gary the rest of the night. I told Gary I'd see him the next night. It felt good sleeping in the next morning. When I arrived that evening, my brother was in very good spirits. His closest friends had spent the afternoon with him.

As I laid back to go to sleep, the nurse came in with medications. She told Gary that she had just found out she was going to have a baby. Gary said, "I'm so happy for you! Congratulations!"

Those were the last words I would ever hear my brother say. Later that night he went into another coma, and he died three days later in the middle of the night. My mother and I were both at his side when he peacefully passed on. I was really going to miss my brother. In a matter of two years I had lost my two best friends, my brother and my dad.

CHAPTER 13

It was probably six months before we made the first big purchase with the settlement money for Brett. We got approval by the court to have the new minivan we had purchased sent off and equipped with a wheelchair conversion, which cost close to twenty-thousand dollars. The conversion consisted of dropping the floor of the van ten inches to provide head room when putting Brett in the van in his wheelchair. There would also be an automatic ramp that would come down on one side. It was so nice when going somewhere with Brett.

We also looked into different types of equipment for inside our home that would aid in the everyday care for Brett, but most of the equipment we were looking at involved major changes inside the house for the equipment. So we started drawing up plans for a totally accessible home.

Even though the real estate market was very good in our small town, I refused to start building until we had a serious contract on our house. We listed our home in early February on a Saturday morning. That same day we already had a serious offer, but it came with one stipulation. The person making the offer would pay our asking price, in cash, as long as we could move out and give possession in three weeks. We also had to give a decision by Monday morning, which was less than thirty-six hours away.

Brenda and I both knew that it was going to be almost impossible to find a place to rent that would fit our needs on such short notice. Brenda called everyone she knew, hoping to find a place for us with no success. On Sunday afternoon, my mother called to see if we had found a place to live. I told her we had not had any luck finding anything. I was very surprised when she asked me if we would consider moving in with her until we finished building our new house. I didn't know what to say. I told her it was a very generous offer but I didn't think it was a very good idea. "Why not?" she asked.

I explained, "We a twenty-four-hour-a-day circus. You won't be able to handle your washing machine and dryer going for hours every day. Also three showers and a bath. All your televisions will be on at the same time, and every light in your house will be on. Brett wakes us up sometimes in the middle of the night needing to go to the bathroom. Gina works late some evenings, and she also goes on dates. I don't think you know what you would be getting yourself into."

My mother said, "I will expect you to pay your share of the expenses."

"Thank you so much for the offer," I said, "but let me talk to Brenda and I'll call you later tonight with an answer."

It was a very nice gesture by my mother. She did have a very nice house, and it was only a few streets up from ours. I had talked her into buying the house about a year after my dad died. It was a very beautiful and spacious home. Also, the lot we were planning to build on was just down the street.

The first thing Brenda told me was that it wasn't a good idea to move in with other family members. I agreed with her. We then talked about our other options... We figured out that we had zero other options. Moving in with my mom was our only choice at that point with such short notice. My mom was bending over backwards trying to make it happen. She was going to let Brenda and me have the master bedroom and bath. Brett would get one extra bedroom, my mom would take the bedroom my brother used, and Gina would take a room downstairs.

Brenda finally told me she didn't think she would be able to live under the same roof with my mother for the six months it would take to build the house, which was how long all the builders we had gotten bids from said it would take to build the house we wanted. I let Brenda continue to give me all her reasons for why this wouldn't work, and then I started to tell her my plans.

"If we accept this offer," I started, "I know I can move us out in three weeks without any problems. We will have to put some of our stuff in storage. The rest we will store in my mom's basement and garage. As soon as we know that this is a for sure deal, we will go get our construction loan and purchase the lot we want to build on. We have the next three weeks to get that part done. By that time it will be the first week of March.

"We are not going to let someone else build our home," I continued. "We are going to be our own general contractor. Brenda, if you let me go with this, I promise you we will be moved into our new home for Gina's high school graduation party in May."

Brenda replied, "Keith, there is no way. Gina's graduation is three months away, and we haven't even bought the lot to build the house. There is no way I'm moving into our new home until it's completely done. You're out of your mind."

I said, "Brenda, if you take care of everything else and let me concentrate totally on the new house, it will happen."

Brenda's last words were, "Whatever! You've already made your decision. But I promise you I will not move in until the home is completely done."

I knew I could get our house built in the time frame I had promised. The whole process was scheduled out in my mind with time to spare. In the end, I got my wish. The next three weeks involved getting moved out and turning our home over to the new owner. I was already looking three or four weeks ahead. We purchased a lot, and I was already going through bids on foundations, framing, plumbing, and electrical.

I finally pulled the trigger on March third and started digging the basement. My foundation guy was going to start the next day on footings and eventually start forming up the basement walls. Everything was going great until a few days of wet weather moved in. It was not a wash out but enough to make the ground soft. My foundation guy had the basement walls ready to pour but said it was too wet to get the concrete trucks out to pour them. I asked him if he had access to a concrete pump. He told me that it wasn't figured in the bid and the cost was probably five hundred dollars. I told him that I would pay for the pump if he would pour the basement walls the next day. He agreed.

Spending the extra money on the concrete pump put everything ahead of schedule. I had my framing crew set up for the seventeenth of March. I had worked with the guy who was going to do the framing for several years. We worked for the same company until he started his own business a few years before. I knew he was fast and also did quality work.

He would put me even further ahead of schedule. His crew would only take six working days to frame our 2,300-square-foot house. With the roof done, I could start my electrician, plumber, and heating and cooling people. Seven days later, the house was ready for drywall.

When I came home after work on Friday, April fourth, I found that my drywall guy had had the entire house stocked for his crew to start the next morning. When we met that night, he told me he had a crew of twelve drywall hangers coming at 7 a.m. in the morning and he would need twenty-four hundred dollars to pay them. I arrived at the house around 9:30 a.m. the next morning. I couldn't believe that they were already fifty percent done. The drywall guy told me they would be finished by noon and asked if I could have everything cleaned up by Monday morning. He also mentioned that I needed to find some type of temporary heat by Monday so he could start taping. I told him that I had two big kerosene heaters that would have the house toasty warm for him to start. He told me it would take at least ten days for him to finish, so I could figure two weeks from that day I would be able to start painting.

I planned on doing the final finish of the house myself. Everything had gone perfectly so far. I had two weeks to purchase the materials needed to complete our new home, including paint, doors, door hardware, closet shelving, mirrors, trim, and hardwood flooring. My boss eventually let me take off three weeks to perform this work. While I worked on the finish inside, work was also being performed outside. Three sides of the house would be bricked, with vinyl siding on the back of the house.

On May eighth, we started moving into our new home, just sixty-seven days after digging the basement. I lost thirty-eight pounds during the building process. We did celebrate Gina's graduation from high school in our beautiful new home as I had promised. I can honestly say it was great to go back to work and get some rest.

Moving into our new home opened up a new world for Brett. Everything was so accessible for him now. A lift system that could carry him from his bed to the toilet and Jacuzzi tub made giving him a bath a breeze. The lift system ran along a rail mounted to the ceiling between his bedroom and bathroom. He also had a vanity sink with space for a wheelchair underneath so he could brush his teeth and wash his hands. All the doorways in the house were three feet wide for easy access with his wheelchair. The three-car garage was designed with extra square footage to allow for the ramp on the van to deploy and leave enough room to access the ramp going into the mud room just off the kitchen.

There also was a family room downstairs with a wet bar, and a bedroom and a full bath for Gina. In order for Brett to have access to the downstairs, a small elevator was designed to come up in the one corner of his bedroom. When the elevator came up from the basement, it lifted a section of floor up to pick Brett up. When the elevator was in the down position, the floor would go back in place, leaving his room with the normal useable square footage as before.

We were so lucky. We had built our home from our design, solving the issues concerning Brett. Our daughter would be leaving for college soon, and I had just started on a major high-rise building. I was the general foreman, and I would be working unbelievable overtime hours, which would help pay for Gina's continuing education. Life was good!

It's so funny how life can be so good and also so bad. I had gone through such a dark stage of life losing my grandfather—the wisest person I would ever know—my father, and my brother in a matter of five years. Going through this in such a short period of time really took a toll on my emotions. But then things got better. Brett received his settlement shortly after that dark period and life started to get good again. The good things were outnumbering the bad.

Our daughter was going to college full time and working at a very popular sports bar in St. Louis. I didn't like the short skirts she had to wear, but the trade-off was the unbelievable tips she made. The main thing was that she was happy! Brett was happy because that was just his way. Brett always had a knack for adapting to different situations around him and making everything good.

Suddenly the pendulum started to move, once again, to the dark side. Brett was fourteen years old. He had been going to the high school for almost three years. Everything had gone pretty good since that big confrontation with the school district. Brett seemed to really like going to the high school. The school district also hired a new director of special services. She happened to be a friend of ours, and we knew she was very well qualified for the job.

Everything had been going great until one day when Brenda was picking up Brett just after lunch time. Brett had an orthodontist appointment. Brenda asked the teacher if she could have Brett's toothbrush to clean his teeth. The class was practicing good hygiene methods by brushing after meals. Brenda followed the teacher back to the room and watched as he pulled a Ziploc bag out of the drawer of his desk. She watched in amazement as he fumbled through probably fifteen tooth brushes, all touching each other. He finally pulled one out and said, "This is Brett's."

Brenda walked back to get Brett, not believing what she had just witnessed. As they drove away from the school to the orthodontist, Brenda couldn't get the picture of the bag of toothbrushes out of her mind. She finally called the school and asked to talk with the principal. When she told him what she had seen, he promised he would immediately investigate what was going on and call her later.

After his investigation, he told Brenda some off-the-wall explanation of what she had seen and that it was all a big mistake. Brenda was even more furious. The next day she called the superintendent of the district. He promised he would do his own investigation, but in the end it came down to Brenda's word against the teacher's. In order to make things right, the school district paid for all the kids to be checked by a doctor. I think this was the last straw for Brenda and me. We had had enough. We both started thinking seriously about moving. This would quickly get put on a back burner due to what was going to happen next.

CHAPTER 14

My job was demanding more and more of my time. I had some of my people starting as early as four in the morning. This meant I needed to be there even earlier to unlock the gates into the jobsite. Some evenings I was not getting home till nine or ten.

One Friday I came home late from work. Brenda was out at some kind of jewelry party, and Gina was home from college for some reason. Brett was on the floor in his room playing video games. I went in and laid on the floor with him, watching him play. I hadn't been with him long and I could already feel myself starting to doze off. I noticed the TV screen was making funny flashes. When I looked at Brett I immediately knew something was drastically wrong. His eyes were making strange back-and-forth deviations, and he was turning a funny color. I got to my knees and started screaming his name. I could tell he wasn't breathing, which really started to freak me out. Gina came running in from the kitchen yelling, "What's wrong, Dad?"

I told her, "Dial nine-one-one! Tell them he's not breathing!"

So many things were going through my mind. I thought my son was dying right before my eyes. Suddenly color started coming back to his face, and I could tell he was breathing again. The ambulance station was only a few blocks from our home, so they arrived in minutes. By the time Gina brought the paramedics into Brett's room, he was starting to come around a bit.

The paramedics told me all Brett's vital signs were okay even though he was still really out of it. They told me that what I witnessed was probably a seizure. A doctor would have to confirm this with tests. They wanted to know if I wanted them to transport him to the hospital. Brett was aware enough to say, "No, Dad, no!"

I didn't know what to do. I was still trembling from what I had just seen. I told Gina to call Doc and see if he would come to the house. He came right over. He agreed it was probably a seizure and we could probably wait until Monday to get Brett to a pediatric neurologist for further testing. Brenda almost had a heart attack when she pulled up to the house with the ambulance in our driveway and Doc's car on the street.

I don't think either one of us slept that night. I will never be able to get the picture of Brett's face and eyes when I first noticed him having the seizure. I can only imagine how other families deal with them. Many children have the same thing and much worse several times a day. I don't think I could ever get used to watching my child go through it on a regular basis.

After several tests the following week, it was determined that Brett had indeed had a seizure. The pediatric neurologist was confident that the problem could be controlled with medication, but Brett would have to be monitored closely with periodic blood tests to see how his body was tolerating the medications. This was just the warm up of our emotions for what we were going to endure in the months ahead.

It had been a little over a year since Brett had last been seen by his orthopedic specialist, Dr. Williams. We were seeing his posture getting worse each month and knew he should go for a checkup before school started in August. The appointment was scheduled for July fifteenth. Brenda asked Donna and the girls to go with them because for some reason she didn't feel comfortable going by herself with Brett. I offered to go, but knowing how busy I was at work then, she offered to ask Donna instead.

When Dr. Williams saw Brett, he could not believe how tall he had gotten or how much weight he had gained. He asked Brenda how things were going, and she told him how concerned she was about his deteriorating posture in the wheelchair. The doctor asked if she had enough time to have X-rays taken of Brett's spine. She was so glad the doctor wanted to X-ray Brett that day. After taking him down to radiology, they came back to the exam room again to talk to the doctor. Dr. Williams asked Brenda and her sister to follow him to another exam room. Donna's girls entertained Brett in the initial exam room while they were away.

Dr. Williams said things were not good. The curvature of Brett's spine, or kyphosis, had gotten much more severe since the last X-rays were performed. He suggested back surgery and the insertion of rods in Brett's back. The Harrington rods would be attached to Brett's spine, thus fixing his posture. Brenda wasn't surprised by the news, but this surgery scared her to death. She told Dr. Williams she would go ahead and schedule the surgery, but if I didn't agree with the decision or had questions after being told, we would call.

Dr. Williams went back into the exam room where Brett was waiting with his cousins and explained everything to him. Brett said he would work real hard at home on his posture if Dr. Williams just canceled the surgery. The doctor assured Brett that he had already given it all he had for fourteen years and it was now time to get him sitting up and looking at the world instead of the floor. Brenda scheduled the surgery for August thirteenth, which was only four weeks away. She had four weeks to get her job and life ready for being home with Brett full time because he would have to lay flat on his back after surgery for six weeks.

When Brenda told me about the surgery, I started to get nauseous. I could see the fear in her face as she told me what was ahead. The doctor would begin by making an incision starting at the base of Brett's neck and extending all the way down his back to the crack of his butt. This wasn't going to be same-day or out-patient surgery. Brett would spend a minimum of five days after surgery in the pediatric ICU and then two or three days in a regular room before going home. Brenda told me if we didn't go through with the surgery, it could really create problems as Brett got older. I couldn't figure out if it was the seizure Brett had or the bad vibes I was getting from Brenda about the surgery, but I was just getting a real bad feeling about what was ahead.

That night we needed to attend a Special Olympics meeting with Brett. It didn't look like Brett would be competing in any events for a long time now. We told them about Brett's upcoming surgery. Knowing that Brett was quite upset over this, the local director offered him twelve tickets to a Cardinal baseball game for the night before his surgery, August twelfth. Brett jumped on that idea! He now had something to look forward to the night before surgery. This sure did help in keeping his mind on the game and not on surgery. Was this God's way of helping Brett cope with the next four weeks?

On July thirtieth, we took Brett in for his pre-op physical and also met with the anesthesiologist. Brett did great, with the exception of drawing his blood for labs. He didn't like that! They explained the surgical process with us. I could see Brenda starting to tear up as we finished. I told her to go into the restroom if she needed to cry so Brett didn't see her. We both needed to put up a front that this was not going to be a big deal. I guess it was starting to hit us as to what was going to happen. How were we ever going to survive with him flat on his back for six weeks?

Our next stop was the Red Cross. Dr. Williams requested Brett to donate his own blood before the surgery because I guess he was going to need blood during or after surgery. When they heard that Brett had already had a bad time with the blood labs earlier, the nurse said she didn't want to put him through any-more. Brenda and I offered to donate for him. I got a little woozy since it was my first time giving blood, but Brenda did fine. We would find out in two days which one of us was compatible with Brett's blood type.

As the big day approached, we had so many things to take care of. We found a hospital bed that we could use for the next several weeks. I would wait till after surgery to pick up the bed just before Brett came home. We planned on putting the bed in our living room so Brett wasn't isolated in his bedroom while he recov-ered. Even though we were just a few days from surgery, I couldn't get the bad feeling out of the pit of my stomach that something was going to go wrong. The only thing that actually gave me com-fort was all the prayers from everyone for Brett.

On the day before the surgery, I planned on leaving work at noon. I hopefully had everything lined out for the unknown time I would be gone. I told my boss that I would not leave my son as long as he was in the pediatric ICU. He told me to take all the time I needed. Brenda was doing the same thing. Maybe going to the ballgame that night would help us all keep our minds off what was about to happen.

Somehow twelve of us fit in the same vehicle for the trip to the ballgame. Brett invited, of course, his mother and father, his sister and her boyfriend, his Aunt Donna, five cousins, and another boyfriend. The whole night went great. I think we actually forgot about the surgery for a few moments and enjoyed the ballgame. The only bad thing was the ballgame went into extra innings. We finally left the ballpark at 10:30 p.m. and wouldn't arrive home till after midnight. The ballgame was still going on when we finally got in bed.

The alarm clock went off at 4 a.m. Brenda wanted Brett to have a good bath because it would be several weeks before he would have another one. We needed to have Brett at the hospital and at patient registration by 6 a.m. The ride to the hospital was very quiet. Usually Brett used an instance like this to con us into buying him something or taking him someplace. Once we arrived at the hospital, everything started to move very quickly. We helped get Brett undressed and into his hospital gown. The nurses then took over, hooking him up to different monitors and starting an IV. They must have given Brett something to take off the edge because he was getting very mellow. I wanted the same thing.

It was Gina's first experience dealing with a situation like this. She did great until the surgical team came to take Brett away to surgery. We each took our turn telling Brett how much we loved him, and we followed him down the hall as they went through the doors into surgery. The three of us turned to walk towards the surgical waiting area in tears. When we arrived at the waiting area, a lady gave us a pager and told us to feel free to get something to eat or go outside for fresh air. They would page us if there was any new information concerning Brett.

Our first page came at 8:15 a.m. telling us that surgery had just begun, and then another one came around 10 a.m. telling us surgery was going well. Brenda's mom showed up to wait with us, followed by one of our close friends, Sue. My mother's minister even stopped by and told us Brett was on the church's prayer chain. I sat and watched doctors come to the surgical waiting area and talk to other people waiting on their loved ones. The area was beginning to thin out.

Shortly after noon, Brenda walked up and asked if someone would call surgery and ask how everything was going. Several minutes passed without a response when suddenly the pager went off. The three of us walked to the information desk to see what the message was. The next words I heard sent chills up and down my spine. We were told that the doctor requested us to meet him in his office as soon as possible.

Red flares went off in my head. I had been through this same situation before with the unfortunate death of my father. All morning we watched other families talk to their doctors in the surgical waiting area. As the three of us walked to the elevator, Brenda glanced at me and said, "I don't like this. Something went wrong!"

I also had a very bad feeling as we entered the elevator. For some reason, from the very beginning after finding out about this surgery, I knew something bad was going to happen. Maybe it was because of the seizure, or the possible complications of this surgery, but I just never liked the idea of it. When the elevator doors opened, I was in panic mode. All I could do was follow Brenda and Gina as we tried to find the doctor's office. When we finally arrived at his personal office, no one was there. We walked back into the hall and could see Dr. Williams with his resident walking towards us.

Expecting bad news, I stayed a few steps behind Brenda and Gina. When we all came together in the hallway, Dr. Williams said the surgery was over. "Brett did excellent! He is in recovery, and it will be awhile before you can see him." Brenda rushed forward and started to hug him. We all thanked him for getting Brett through this.

Once Brett arrived in the ICU, we were allowed to stay with him as long as we wanted. Brenda and I stayed by his side the whole time he was there. Brett was really out of it the first few days with all the medications they were giving him for the pain. I watched the ICU nurses very closely as they cared for Brett lying flat on his back the first night. Brenda had lined up a room at the Ronald McDonald House so she could get some rest. When she arrived in the morning, I went home to clean up and also get some rest.

I quickly came back to the hospital after Brenda called me and said Brett was really crabby and running a 102 degree fever. They told us this was normal after this type of surgery. Brett had many visitors stop in that day to check on his condition even though they couldn't see him because he was still in the ICU. That night, before Brenda went back to the Ronald McDonald House for some sleep, she told me that she had a gut feeling something wasn't right with Brett. When I asked her what it was, she just told me to keep a close eye on him overnight and if something happened to call her immediately.

After she told me about her gut feeling, I watched Brett very closely through the night. The nurses were in and out all night, none saying anything was unusual about his condition. At 5:30 a.m., some of the medical students, interns, and resident doctors started filtering in on their normal rounds. They all seemed to think Brett was doing great. I talked at great length with a young medical student who witnessed Brett's surgery. He went into great detail as he explained what Brett went through on the operating table. When Brenda arrived about an hour later, I told her everything seemed good with Brett's condition.

She still thought something wasn't right. I told her everything was fine and to start thinking positively. I told Brenda I needed to go home and check on the house, clean up, and get some rest. I felt guilty leaving Brenda when she had such bad feelings about Brett, but I knew I needed to get away and get some rest. I was halfway home when my cell phone started ringing. It was Brenda. She told me she really had a bad feeling that something was about to happen with Brett. I told her that Brett was in an intensive care unit and receiving the best care possible. She started crying and asked me to turn around and come back. She told me something was wrong.

I had no choice but turn around and head back to the hospital. When I arrived back at the room, I found Dr. Williams talking to Brenda and Brett. I walked around the bed and stood next to the doctor as he examined Brett. The ICU nurses were working in the background when Brett exploded like a volcano and projectile vomited all over Dr. Williams. The vomit hit the doctor right in the middle of his white coat. I will never forget Dr. Williams telling the nurses, "Ladies get this gentleman rolled over before he aspirates!"

After this episode, we were told that the nausea was caused by the pain medications. They made adjustments to his pain medications, and things started to get better. Brett finally came out of the ICU after six days and was put into a normal hospital room. When Dr. Williams came in that afternoon to check on Brett, he told us that he knew Brett would have the same care or better if he was released to go home.

The doctor was correct. Once we had Brett back at home, we became his cooks, servants, nurses and doctors. Brett loved all the attention from family and friends stopping in around the clock to check on him. The next six weeks passed by quickly, and Brett was back into a normal routine by the holidays.

As the new year started, we all began to get into a normal routine again. My boss told me to work whatever hours it took to keep the job on schedule. I was starting to wear down from all the overtime until one evening Gina's boyfriend Tim came by the house unexpectedly.

Gina and Tim had been going out off and on since we allowed her to start dating. Tim started his own custom cabinet business just out of high school and designed and had installed the kitchen cabinets, dining bar, and bathroom vanities in the house we built. He gave us the boyfriend discount, which was over and beyond what we had expected. He did a fabulous job. The only problem was after we moved into our new home and had Gina's graduation party, they broke up. I felt so bad after all he had done for us. Plus, I really liked the guy.

A few months after they broke up, they got back together again. The reason Tim stopped in unexpectedly was because he needed to ask me a question. He asked, "May I have your permission to ask Gina to marry me?" Brenda must of known something was going on because she came running out yelling, "Oh my God!"

I told him, "You have my blessing under one condition. You

need to promise me she will finish college. I will pay for the rest of her education, but I want her to finish what she's started."

Tim replied, "I promise."

Plans were quickly made. We had the church and a place for the reception. The next step was how many people were going to be invited. Living in a small town and Brenda practically knowing everyone in the county after working for Doc nineteen years, I might as well have put an ad in the local paper to save money on invitations. I cringed when I finally got to see the invitation list. The four of us were sitting at the dining room table.

I asked Brenda, "How many people?"

Brenda made a funny face and said, "Five hundred."

"Are you out of your mind!"

Gina jumped in and said, "Dad, a lot of it is Tim's family, who live out of town. Not everybody who is invited will come."

"We can't handle that many people at the church," I said. "The church only holds three hundred people, three hundred and fifty at the max. Maybe it would work if we only invite three hundred to the wedding and five hundred to the reception."

Brenda said, "You can't do that Keith."

Gina also jumped in and said, "Dad, it will work. Don't worry about it, everything will work out fine."

I said, "Gina! You can't invite five hundred people to a church that only holds three hundred. It won't work!"

I looked at Tim, thinking maybe he would surely see my reasoning for why this was a problem. "Do you see what I'm saying here? What do you think we need to do?"

Tim looked at me and said, "I guess we need a bigger church."

A few days later, I came home from work and collapsed on

the bed. Brenda came in a few minutes later and said she had bad news. I looked up at her hoping she hadn't invited more people to the wedding. She told me about something that happened at school that day. It was very bad. She assured me it didn't involve Brett.

I put my hands on my head and said, "I can't take it anymore. It's never going to end. It's time to move on. When I come home tomorrow night, I hope there's a for-sale sign in our yard. The next day when I pulled in the driveway, the first thing I saw was a for-sale sign.

Afterword

Sixteen years have passed since we made the decision to sell our home and move to a community more receptive to our son's needs. This in no way reflects upon the many friends and fine people we left behind. Marshalltown is one of the finest places to raise a family in the USA.

So many things have changed over the years. Gina and Tim did get married. I think 495 of the five hundred invited to the church did show up. It was extremely crowded, but everything turned out great. Since then, Gina and Tim have blessed us with two wonderful grandsons, Isaac and Alex. Brenda and I treasure every moment we get to spend with them.

I was very concerned about how Brenda would deal with her new surroundings after our move. Brenda had always lived in the country. Even though we were not moving all the way into the city, it was still going to be a big adjustment for her. I knew she wouldn't have any problems finding a job in the medical field with all her experience.

For some reason, she had other thoughts. I sensed she wanted to try something different. While Brett recovered from the surgery on his spine, Brenda started a side business selling candles to earn money for Christmas shopping. She enjoyed this work so much that she decided to make it her full-time occupation. Even though I was very skeptical about her new business venture, I still supported her decision. I just wanted her to be happy.

She had a very difficult time getting her business going at first. After the first year, Brenda's hard work started to pay off, and seven years later, the direct sales company she worked for promoted her to regional vice president. During this wild ride, Brenda earned eleven fabulous vacations for the both of us. I was very proud of her.

Brett's life dramatically changed after we moved. The high school he attended was very new and accessible. It was a pleasure watching our son flourish in his new surroundings. Brett started getting involved in many different activities around the community. One of Brett's new activities was with a group that met every so often and bowled a few games. One Sunday afternoon as I was dropping Brett off to bowl with his new friends, something very unfortunate happened. As I started rolling Brett into the building, we met most of the group walking out. I asked one of the other fathers what was going on. He told me that there had been a confrontation inside with the manager of the bowling alley. Apparently, the manager of the establishment told one of the parents in our group that a lot of his Sunday business was family parties and birthday celebrations for younger children. The manager didn't think all the people having parties should have to watch a bunch of handicapped kids trying to bowl. One father in the group had to be restrained by several other people.

Sadly, the worst thing about this situation was the kids had to listen to this jerk and his inappropriate thoughts. Brett was sixteen years old and, just like all his friends, wanted to do fun things like anyone else. This was one of the biggest challenges I personally needed to fix. Brett wanted to do new things every day, and I was always coming up with excuses for why it wouldn't work. The main reason we moved was to give Brett a life, and I was too stubborn to let him enjoy it.

Brenda and I had been season ticket holders for several years at the University of Missouri. Brett asked me a thousand times to take him to a football game. I was really good at coming up with different excuses, but my best was that there were too many steps to our seats. When Brenda and I originally purchased our season tickets, it was supposed to be a way for us to get away for a day with some of our friends. At first, it was very fun for the both of us. I knew Brenda never saw the football after the kickoff, but she loved the tailgating before and after the games. Just after kickoff, Brenda would get up and say it was too cold and she was going to the mall. After several years, my patience started to wear very thin.

One day, as a big game approached against the Oklahoma Sooners, I asked Brenda if she was planning on going. She told me she would let me know later in the week. Brett happened to hear this and said, "Please, Dad, please take me."

I looked at Brett and said, "I'll tell you what, buddy. If I can exchange our seats for wheelchair seats, you're in."

I called the university the next day and they told me there was an accessible seating area just ten rows behind our existing seats. It's so funny how I never noticed it before. I will never forget Brett's face when I told him he was going.

When the day of the game finally arrived, Brett was as excited as I had ever seen. We arrived at the stadium mid-morning for an early evening kickoff. The accessible parking lot was right next to the stadium. The atmosphere was amazing as the two of us tailgated all day. Brett was in heaven. I can't remember him ever being so happy. At one point I slipped away for a few minutes to go to the bathroom, and when I came back I noticed Brett had already made a new friend. His name was Mike. We talked for hours getting to know each other.

It was a very good game that evening, but Mizzou eventually came out on the losing end after a trick play by Oklahoma. I will always remember Brett looking up at me as I pushed him in his wheelchair through the parking lot. He said, "Dad, from here on out it's you and me! Mom is never coming back. It's you and me!"

Something happened to me that day. On one hand, I knew I had created a monster. On the other hand, it was probably the best day I had ever experienced with my son. I think when you care for someone on a twenty-four hour basis, you start forgetting about the actual person who is right in front of you. I finally figured out that my son shared the same passion I did—sports.

I could tell a thousand stories of how Brett has changed my life. After I took Brett to his first football game, I switched our tickets to accessible seating. Over the next several years, Brett and I never missed a game. We have also traveled to several bowl games over the years, most recently the Cotton Bowl in January of 2014. Because of Brett, we have made close friends with people from all over the state of Missouri and other parts of the country. One day while we were tailgating before a game against the Longhorns of Texas, I helped an older gentleman back his car into the parking space next to ours even though I noticed his license plate was from Texas. About thirty minutes later, I noticed the old guy was just sitting in his car. I knocked on his window and told him we had plenty of extra food and drinks. He smiled and got out of his vehicle, immediately walking back to the trunk of his car. He pulled out a University of Texas hat and t-shirt and then gave the items to Brett.

Everyone tailgating around us must have been looking on because they started yelling at Brett, "No, don't take it!" Brett held the shirt and hat high into the air, loving all the attention he was getting. The gentleman's name was John. He talked to Brett for several minutes and then walked up to me. I thanked him for his generosity and told him to help himself to our snacks and food. John told me he had never missed a Texas football game, home or away, in over forty years. He then pulled out a business card and handed it to me. He said, "The next time Missouri plays Texas in Austin, call me. I will have tickets for you."

I said, "That's a very kind offer, John. Thank you so much. I know if I call you in a year or two, you're never going to remember me, though."

John said, "You're probably right, I won't remember you. I'll remember your son."

On Christmas Day of that year, Brett received a phone call from John wishing him happy holidays and a happy birthday. What a wonderful person.

Shortly after we moved to our new location, we talked Brenda's parents and my mother into moving closer to us. Vicky and Jim, Brenda's parents, moved only ten minutes from our house, and my mother was just over five minutes away. It was nice having them so close. Sadly, a few years later Jim died in October of 2002. Brett loved spending time with his Paw Paw.

It's hard to describe how Brett has handled death over the years. He never really shows any type of emotions after the loss of a loved one. I'll never forget what happened at the cemetery during the burial service for his grandfather. The ground was soft and wet when we arrived at the cemetery. We parked the van as close as we could to the grave site and left Brett in the van with the sliding door open so he could hear the service. Because Jim had served during the Korean War, his burial included a military service. Just after "Taps" was played, the honor guard started firing shots into the air. When the gunfire stopped, Brett yelled out from the van, "Hey, what are you guys doing to him!" Everyone at the service busted out laughing. Jim would have loved it.

Around a year later, about the time Brenda started getting over the death of her father, she found out her mother had cancer. Vicky died ninety-one days later in January of 2004. Brenda started going through the dark days I had dealt with several years earlier after the death of my father and brother.

Time started to pass by very quickly. Brett graduated high school in 2005 at the age of twenty-one. Brenda called around, trying to find some type of job Brett could do instead of being home watching TV all day. She wasn't having much luck. One day, Brett was supposed to meet a group at a new movie theater that had just opened five minutes from our house. When Brenda took him into the movie theater, Brett looked around and said, "I would love to work here, Mom."

The manager of the theater happened to hear him. He walked up to Brett and said, "We would love to have you as an employee."

Brett has been working at the theater for ten years now. One of the days he works is usually very busy because people can get a senior citizen discount. One of the managers told me that the home office gets periodic emails that Brett is the reason they go to that theater. I'm so proud of him.

In 2010, I took my thirty-year pension at the age of fifty-one and retired. Brenda and I reversed roles, and I started taking care of Brett and everything around the house. It was a full-time job, and I loved it. Brett and I started doing a lot of traveling all over the country. Sometimes it was just Brett and me, sometimes Brenda joined us, and a lot of times my mother accompanied Brett and me, too.

We have a new member of the family that sticks to Brett like glue everywhere he goes. His name is William, and he is Brett's service dog. William is a standard poodle and probably one of the smartest dogs I've ever seen. He is trained to pick up things Brett drops during the day, and he has also become a great companion. William doesn't like when strangers get too close to Brett. He has never barked or growled at anyone in public, but always places himself between the stranger and Brett. I think if anyone tried to harm Brett in any way, the dog would act accordingly.

One day, I came into the house after working in the yard for a few hours to check on Brett and get a drink. When I walked into Brett's room, William jumped up and started barking at me. Thinking he might need to go outside, I opened the door. He stood in the doorway and started jumping, and then he bumped me with his nose. I knew he was trying to tell me something. William followed me upstairs and kept making whining sounds. As I walked to the refrigerator to get some tea, he started bumping me again. I looked at him, trying to figure out what he trying to tell me. William was looking down at the floor. I looked down and noticed a bumblebee on the floor at my feet. I finally figured out William had noticed the big bee crawling on my shirt and had tried to tell me.

Towards the end of 2008, Brett developed a bad ear infection. The infection in his left ear was like many of the others he had experience in the last year. This one wouldn't go away, though. Our family doctor suggested Brett be seen by an ear, nose, and throat specialist. After the specialist examined the infected ear, he told Brenda that he thought Brett might have a tumor behind his eardrum. He wanted an immediate CAT scan to confirm his findings. The CT scan did confirm the doctor's diagnosis.

Surgery was scheduled for the first week of January in 2009. The doctor told us he was ninety-nine percent sure it was a benign tumor. When the day of surgery arrived, we were all very nervous, just like we were at all the other major surgeries Brett had endured. Gina helped keep her brother calm as he was prepped for surgery. Once again, we were all overcome with emotion as they wheeled Brett to surgery. Brenda's older sister, her husband, and my mother waited with us during the five-hour surgery.

The doctor had to make an incision completely around the back of Brett's left ear to access the tumor. Once he removed the tumor, he also had to rebuild part of the eardrum. Brett came out of surgery late that afternoon. Unbelievably, we brought Brett home late that evening.

Unfortunately in July of 2014, the tumor reappeared. The doctor once again ordered a CT scan on Brett's left ear. Brenda and I figured Brett would once again need surgery. When we took Brett back to the specialist, he surprised us with very distressing news. The doctor informed us that the tumor was back. He also told us that this one looked like it was attached to the brain. He said that this surgery was much more than he could handle, and he set us up with another doctor more specialized in the type of surgery Brett needed.

Brenda and I were both emotional messes the next few days. When we finally arrived at the office of the new doctor, we feared the worse. The doctor was amused when he came into the room to examine Brett. William was sprawled out on the floor next to Brett's wheelchair, sound asleep. The doctor looked at the CT scan and said he wanted Brett's hearing checked. He told us after Brett was tested that he would talk to us in his office.

When we sat down with the doctor in his office we were prepared for bad news. He told us that the hearing tests showed the new tumor had not done any nerve damage. He told us that it would be three weeks before he could fit Brett into his surgery schedule. He also told us that he would make changes to the ear canal and eardrum to make sure the tumor would never come back. Knowing the last surgery had been over five hours in duration, we figured this one would be much longer. The doctor explained he would need to basically remove the outer part of the ear, just like the previous surgery, to access the tumor. When we asked him if we should be prepared for a few days in the hospital, he chuckled and told us, at the most, the surgery would last ninety minutes and Brett should be heading home by late afternoon. As it turned out, the surgery only lasted about an hour. Brett was home by mid-afternoon.

Brenda and I have devoted thirty-one years to caring for our son around the clock, seven days a week. Recently, we have discussed future plans of setting Brett up in a group living situation. In the unfortunate case that something happened to the two of us, we don't want this burden to fall into Gina's lap. We have several ideas on what we plan on doing. Right now we call it our five-year plan.

One of my biggest concerns regarding Brett involves his communication when something is bothering him. Brett has an unbelievable tolerance to pain. He also has an extreme fear of hospitals. All of his experiences in hospitals have involved major surgeries. I'm very concerned that someday a health issue is going to arise and Brett's going to try to hold back whatever the issue is.

My worst fear came to life. A few days ago, William and I went to pick up Brett from work at the movie theater. I parked right in front of the movie theater because it was very cold and I didn't want to take his wheelchair through all the salt on the parking lot.

When William and I entered through the doors, I said hello to a couple of Brett's coworkers behind the ticket desk, and William unexpectedly jumped forward a couple of times towards Brett. He even started pulling me towards Brett, who was probably fifty feet from us. All my concentration was on the dog because he wasn't listening to my commands. As we approached Brett, I looked up and immediately knew something wasn't right.

William started doing things I had never seen before. He kept bumping Brett's leg with his nose, then started licking his fingers. I had been so focused on what the dog was doing, but my attention finally turned back to Brett. I said, "Brett, what's wrong?"

He leaned way back in his wheelchair and replied, "It's been a long day."

Again, I said, "Brett, I know something is wrong. Please tell me!"

Brett again leaned back and said, "I'm fine!"

After I loaded Brett into the van and started driving home, I kept looking into my rearview mirror, watching Brett turn his head side to side in obvious pain while the freaking dog stood on the backseat licking his ears. I knew something was seriously wrong. I looked down and noticed I was doing sixty-five in a forty-five zone. I didn't care.

After I whipped through our driveway and into the garage, I had Brett inside the house within seconds. I remember yelling out to Brenda as I brought him through the kitchen and into the upstairs living room. Brenda came dashing up the stairs, wondering what was happening. Once she looked at Brett, she knew something was seriously wrong.

Brenda quickly got a cool washcloth and placed it on Brett's head. She then looked down at our son and said she would be right back. All I could do was place the cool washcloth around my son's head. A few minutes later, Brenda came running back and told Brett she had called a friend to come over and check his blood pressure. Confused, I looked up at Brenda. With very wide eyes, I watched her silently mouth nine-one-one. In a way, I was relieved she had called.

Brenda and I stood over our son the next few minutes, wondering when the emergency crew would arrive. When I started to hear the sirens, I walked outside to greet the paramedics. I was very surprised that a fire truck had also been dispatched to our house. Everyone followed me in. The paramedics immediately took Brett's blood pressure, which was 178 over 110. They tried to ask Brett what was hurting him. Brett was becoming very agitated and said his head hurt.

One paramedic stood up and told Brenda and me that they needed to transport our son to the hospital. Brett started to throw a fit. We told him that the hospital would give him medicine to help whatever was hurting him. I asked the guys if William could stay with Brett, and they told us his service dog could also ride in the ambulance. Once they had Brett loaded and secured, William and I quickly followed and sat down next to Brett. William watched very closely as the paramedic started checking Brett's vitals. As we pulled out of the subdivision, the paramedic called the hospital with information on Brett and advised them the patient had a service dog. We arrived at the hospital in five minutes.

I could hear people talking about William as we entered the exam room. Two nurses were waiting for Brett and started hooking him up to different equipment. A few minutes later, Brenda arrived and told me Gina was on her way, too. Brett looked so tense lying on the hospital stretcher. His toes and feet were both curled in pain from whatever he was experiencing. When the doctor finally came in, he started asking Brett what was going on. The doctor looked to be in his late sixties, if I were to guess. Brett told him his head hurt. The doctor carefully listened to Brett's heart and chest. He told nurse to get Brett hooked up to an EKG. I looked at Brenda and shook my head.

Once the nurse had placed all the stickers in different spots on Brett's body, she started hooking up the leads from the machine. The doctor then wanted to listen to Brett's lungs from the back side. I pulled Brett forward while the doctor listened to several different spots. The doctor looked at the EKG and said, "What the heck." He asked the nurse if the battery was getting low on the machine. He then grabbed a plug and plugged it into a receptacle behind Brett's bed. My heart almost stopped when I heard the doctor say, "That's not good."

The doctor looked at Brenda and me and said, "This isn't a heart attack. Your son's heart is racing between 130 and 150 beats per minute. I believe Brett has an infection that has dehydrated his body, making his heart race like this. If I were to guess, I believe he might have pneumonia. I could hear a few squeaks while I listened to his lungs. I want to get a chest X-ray to confirm this, though. For right now, I want to start an antibiotic IV, along with another bag to pump fluids to help rehydrate his system."

Brett asked, "Can I please go home tonight?"

The doctor replied, "I will do everything I can to get you home tonight, but there is a possibility you might have to stay."

I asked, "Can you please give something to relax him?"

The doctor said he would order something right away.

The chest X-ray did confirm Brett had pneumonia. Brenda and I couldn't figure it out. He never showed any symptoms. Brett ended up having to spend the night in the hospital. I stayed with him and watched his vitals come back to normal by morning. The house doctor wanted another X-ray of Brett's chest before she would discharge him later that afternoon.

Brett was finally released late that afternoon, feeling much better. The doctor wanted Brett to continue with an antibiotic for the next ten days. As we pulled into our driveway, I said, "Home sweet home, Brett."

Brett leaned forward and responded, "You guys are the best! You take such good care of me. I love you both so much!"

Several times each and every day, Brett will tell Brenda and me how much he loves us, thanking us for taking care of him. Brenda and I often wonder how come God chose us to be so lucky to be the parents of a special needs child. We are blessed!

CPSIA information can be obtained at www.ICGtesting.com
Printed in the USA
BVOW05s1552120715

408382BV00010B/200/P